T0301181

"Some of our greatest lessons result from experiencing shame if we are able to learn from the emotion. McKay, Greenberg, and Fanning illuminate the foundation of shame in defectiveness schemas; and the negative, automatic thoughts and coping mechanisms that accompany this behavioral pattern. They help readers recognize the thoughts associated with the experience of shame in defectiveness schemas, including hypersensitivity to criticism, blame, comparison, and rejection. Through facilitating the clarification of values and employing mindfulness practices, they guide readers to an awareness of the emotion and its accompanied sensations, thoughts, and urges—skillfully demonstrating an approach that leads to accepting feelings, having self-compassion, and responding in new ways."

—**Mary Lamia, PhD**, clinical psychologist, professor, and coauthor of
The Upside of Shame

"For anyone struggling with depression, McKay, Greenberg, and Fanning have combined in one amazing book the key to understanding your illness and the method of unlocking its grip on your life. The authors have created a step-by-step process to rewrite negative self-beliefs, change feelings of defectiveness, live a meaningful life, and develop self-compassion. Surely anyone who follows their guidance will experience a significant life improvement."

—**Jeffrey C. Wood, PsyD**, psychologist, and coauthor of *The Dialectical Behavior Therapy Skills Workbook* and *The New Happiness*

"An incredibly powerful, well-written, and important book for addressing the feelings of inadequacy, defectiveness, shame, unlovability, and hopelessness that often come with depression. Using techniques from acceptance and commitment therapy (ACT), this workbook offers valuable strategies for addressing childhood wounds, rewriting your story, and moving toward individual values and goals. It gives readers a critical opportunity to change the way they see themselves—and to subsequently change their lives."

—**Rachel Zoffness, PhD**, assistant clinical professor at the University of California, San Francisco; chair of the American Association of Pain Psychology; and author of *The Pain Management Workbook* and *The Chronic Pain and Illness Workbook for Teens*

"At last, a book that brings light to what most clinicians intuitively understand: the relationship between shame and depression. The authors clarify the origins and maintenance of depression by identifying and deconstructing defective schemas. Complex concepts are conveyed clearly and illustrated through case studies. Exercises and worksheets prompt the client to identify triggers and to reframe thoughts. Psychotherapists and laypersons will find this book an essential tool in treating depression

—**Cynthia Boyd, PhD**, forensic neuropsychologist in independent practice in La Jolla, CA

"When someone has the belief that they are defective in some way, it can lead to a fear of getting close to others, often resulting in loneliness, depression, and shame. If you feel this way, you are not alone. This workbook will help you identify what is standing in the way of believing you are worthy of the love and acceptance that you deserve."

—**Michelle Skeen, PsyD**, author of *Love Me, Don't Leave Me*; and coauthor of *Just As You Are*

"Thoughts related to shame and 'being defective' affect a multitude of people; for many sufferers the tendency is to shut down, hide, isolate, disconnect from others, and stop living life. Who wants that? In this workbook, the authors introduce readers to skills derived from ACT to unpack these behaviors, stop being trapped by those narratives, and start living a fulfilling life. This is a workbook that is written in plain language, with lot of examples and specific skills to put into action. I highly recommend it!"

—**Patricia E. Zurita Ona, PsyD**, author of *The ACT Workbook for Teens with OCD* and *Living Beyond OCD Using Acceptance and Commitment Therapy*, director of the East Bay Behavior Therapy Center, and fellow of the Association for Contextual Behavioral Science

The
ACT
WORKBOOK
for
DEPRESSION
& SHAME

**OVERCOME THOUGHTS OF DEFECTIVENESS
& INCREASE WELL-BEING USING
ACCEPTANCE & COMMITMENT THERAPY**

MATTHEW McKAY, PhD
MICHAEL JASON GREENBERG, PsyD
PATRICK FANNING

New Harbinger Publications, Inc.

Publisher's Note

This publication is designed to provide accurate and authoritative information in regard to the subject matter covered. It is sold with the understanding that the publisher is not engaged in rendering psychological, financial, legal, or other professional services. If expert assistance or counseling is needed, the services of a competent professional should be sought.

NEW HARBINGER PUBLICATIONS is a registered trademark of New Harbinger Publications, Inc.

Distributed in Canada by Raincoast Books

Copyright © 2020 by Matthew McKay, Michael Jason Greenberg, and Patrick Fanning
    New Harbinger Publications, Inc.
    5674 Shattuck Avenue
    Oakland, CA 94609
    www.newharbinger.com

Cover design by Amy Shoup

Acquired by Catharine Meyers

Edited by Jennifer Eastman

All Rights Reserved

Library of Congress Cataloging-in-Publication Data on file

Printed in the United States of America

24   23   22

10   9   8   7   6   5   4   3

Contents

Chapter 1

Your Defectiveness Schema

If you're reading this book, there is a good chance that feelings of defectiveness and depression have been a part of your life. You've been living with thoughts that you're flawed somehow, unworthy of other people's respect, and no one could ever care about you. It might feel as if you've been living your life behind a cold and abrasive mask. This mask is heavy and burdensome in its crude design. Its weight saps energy, motivation, and desire from your body. Behind the mask, you experience the world from your own portable prison, far removed from the experiences of love, admiration, and connection that seem natural and easy to those living a "normal" life. With its oppressive and isolating nature, this weight has inspired you to try to free yourself from its grasp. For a while, things might have seemed like they were looking up for you—starting a new relationship, getting a new job, achieving some success. But in the end, it was only a matter of time before pain, rejection, and failure reminded you once again why you wore the mask in the first place. And each time you see that happy couple, read that positive status update, or hear that cheerful reassurance—"Everyone feels sad at times" or "You just need to be positive"—you are reminded of how disconnected you are from the "normal" human experience. Perhaps it's gotten to the point that you feel like nobody will ever truly love you.

If this sounds like you, maybe you've already given up on ever feeling "normal," and you have resigned yourself to a life of feeling unfulfilled, depressed, and alone. But maybe you're reading this book because there is a part of you that wants to be freed from the crushing weight of depression. Maybe you picked up this book because you've decided it was time to approach your depression from a different perspective, and start your journey toward living a life of acceptance and empowerment, in which you can make decisions that are consistent with a life you value. If you have come to the point in your life when you are no longer content with hiding behind the heavy mask of depression and defectiveness, this book is written for you.

This book is different. It was written to teach you the techniques of mindfulness (the ability to nonjudgmentally notice your experience) and what is known, in acceptance and commitment therapy, as "defusion" (the ability to separate yourself from your thoughts and recognize your thoughts for what they are). Odds are that the thoughts that your depression and your sense of defectiveness generate in you are insistent and overwhelming. Mindfulness and defusion help you learn to look at those thoughts differently, so as to reduce their overwhelming nature and open space to act differently.

This book will also teach you how to recognize your values, what really matters to you, as opposed to what defectiveness and depression tell you that you can or can't do. And it guides you through exposure—a psychological intervention to reduce the depression, fear, shame, and anger that currently control and limit your behavior. Finally, it gives you concrete steps to engage in acceptance and commitment therapy (ACT) values-based behavior, and it shows you how to develop a more detached observer self to replace self-defeating behaviors. In the following chapters, you will learn to utilize mindfulness, defusion, and exposure as a way to stand tall against the depression that has enslaved you to suffering. With your newfound resilience, you will apply personal, value-driven behaviors to regain control of your life and fortify yourself to whatever challenges the future may hold.

Before you learn how to tackle your depressive symptoms, it is important to learn why your depression came along in the first place. In order to answer this question, you need to understand how one of the fundamental attributes to your development has created a script that colors every aspect of your perception. Perhaps without even knowing it, you have been wearing a tinted pair of glasses that changed the way you see yourself, others, and the world around you.

Schemas

Much like the actors and actresses of movies and theatrical productions, we play out the acts of our lives by reading different scripts. From an early age, we start composing our individual scripts based on the relationships and experiences we have in the world around us. Tasked with filling in the numerous blank pages of our character, we engage in the exploration of cause and effect, translating the feedback we receive from our parents, our peers, and the people we meet into core themes that continue to guide us throughout our development. Positive experiences often result in the development of a script of trust and self-confidence, and negative or traumatic events can damage our self-conception and our relationships with others. Either way, whether positive or negative, our scripts become the database for our behaviors, relationships, attachments, and motivations.

During the development of your script, you were exposed to a negative or traumatic event that made you feel unlovable, broken, or rejected. Imagine what would happen if that negative event was used as a template for future events, behaviors, and relationships. According to the psychologist Jeffrey Young (Young et al., 2003), this is how people develop schemas. *Schemas* are powerful core beliefs and feelings that you accept and live by without question. From its conception, your schema has played a pivotal role in your navigation of the world, helping you make sense of it; it functions like an unspoken universal law for you. And all your schema needs to grow stronger and guide your behavior is a cue from your environment to play its part—some sort of stimulus in your environment that activates it. In these moments, your schema wields powerful control, bringing forth in you myriad fears, negative emotions, and dysfunctional thoughts, and making you feel, for instance, defective.

Because it is integral to helping you make sense of the world, the schemas you develop will often remain throughout the course of your adult life. Your schema knows how to fight for its own survival, even if you get extensive therapy and have incredible life success. It is capable of guiding your behaviors, thoughts, and relationships in a way such that the end result always confirms its validity. Sometimes subtle in its effect, but powerful in its widespread application, your schema is incredibly resilient. Schemas have also been shown to be a significant contributor to depressive symptoms (McGinn et al., 2005). The particular schema you have is one called a "defectiveness schema."

Defectiveness Schema

A defectiveness schema is a core belief that makes you feel internally flawed in some critical way. It leads you to feel that if people get close to you or see your significant defects, they will reject you and withdraw from you. Your feelings of defectiveness might be attached to your perceptions of private flaws (selfishness, angry impulses, unacceptable sexual desires) or to public flaws (in the form of undesirable physical appearance or social awkwardness). Because of your defectiveness schema, you might be hypersensitive to any form of criticism, blame, comparison, or rejection from people around you. It might even feel as if, should anyone see the *real* you, they would find you to be inferior and unlovable. Through facilitating the feeling of being broken or bad, your schema also prevents you from forming satisfying relationships or stable attachments.

The term "schemas" was developed by the psychologist Jeffrey Young (Young et al., 2003), who noted that they tend to take root when a person is exposed to significant, often traumatic events. Young identified five domains in which people tend to hold sets of core beliefs that control their perceptions, thoughts, and feelings about situations they're in, but only one—disconnection and rejection—is used in this treatment. People with schemas in this domain believe that their needs for stability, safety, nurturance, love, and belonging will not be met, and so they avoid relationships altogether, submit to relationships that confirm their feelings of defectiveness (and are often abusive and destructive), or jump from one relationship to the next so as to ensure no one ever gets to see the real them. They also find themselves struggling with depression.

Like the other schemas, defectiveness usually takes root when an individual is exposed to traumatic events (often those with strong themes of rejection and criticism) during their childhood. Through either one single event or multiple events over a long period of time, defectiveness characterizes a powerful belief that can prevent you from forming nourishing relationships, succeeding in life, or experiencing happiness. Once you internalize these feelings of defectiveness, your schema will produce chronic negative thoughts about yourself, your relationships, and the world around you. Your defectiveness schema has likely had a huge impact on your life. But you are not alone in struggling with this. Consider Lilly's story.

• Lilly

Lilly is a thirty-two-year-old woman who has been suffering with crippling depression and anxiety throughout most of her life. If you were to see Lilly walking around in public, you might just take her for someone who is extremely shy and introverted. She doesn't like to make eye contact and speaks at a volume barely above a whisper. Lilly lives in a shared house with two individuals with whom she rarely socializes, spending most of her waking life buried in her room. Lilly had attended college for a couple of years, but eventually dropped out; she felt a lot of shame and self-criticism when she talked to people, and it was just too stressful to be social there. She opted to complete certification as a lab technician instead, and she has been working in a lab for the last six months, processing blood samples, hidden away from the social exchanges of the outside world.

Lilly has been in two long-term relationships in her adult life, both with anxious and hypercritical individuals who eventually ended the relationship when Lilly would engage in isolation. Lilly has been in therapy for the past five years and has been taking Zoloft for over a year to help moderate her depression. While therapy has helped her make some improvements in her ability to take care of daily activities and work-related goals, Lilly's depression and avoidance of social interactions persist, making every day another difficult obstacle to surmount.

Lilly grew up in a single-parent home, with her mother going to school and working two jobs just to keep a roof over the heads of Lilly and her younger brother. Lilly's mother was rarely home, and on the few occasions that she was, she was rarely consistent with her love and attention toward Lilly. She made it a frequent point to remind her children that "kids who don't make the grades and do their homework end up on the street."

As the eldest child, Lilly's punishment for getting poor grades or losing things at school, which occurred on a frequent basis, was to be made an example of, a cautionary tale for her younger brother. Sometimes her punishments would also involve physical beatings, being locked into her room, or going the day without food to "experience what it's like to be homeless." As motivated and intent toward success as Lilly was, she always seemed to struggle with maintaining her concentration on tasks for extended periods of time. She would also drift off into daydreams, lose or forget important materials that she needed for class, or make careless mistakes in her homework. Each time this occurred, Lilly would be punished.

By the time Lilly started attending high school, she was convinced that her mother would never show her love. Her brother made the top marks she could only dream of achieving, but Lilly remained deficient. Eventually, one of Lilly's teachers saw the effort that she made behind her timid demeanor and presented her concerns to the school counselor. Lilly was tested and found to meet criteria for ADHD. Lilly was started on medication in her junior year of high school, and while her grades demonstrated notable improvement, Lilly remained entrenched in her defectiveness. She continued to avoid most social interactions, especially those with her mother, and focused her efforts on finding ways to escape the painful sting of shame that accompanied her wherever she went. Finally, at the age of seventeen, Lilly left her small town in the Midwest to attend college on the West Coast. While she had finally achieved freedom away from her family, her defectiveness schema was entrenched and well developed, ensuring that her history of abuse had a lasting impact on her perceptions of the world and the relationships around her.

As you can see from Lilly's story, when a defectiveness schema sets in, we engage in certain behaviors to cope—like avoiding other people and the ways we feel they judge us, or avoiding certain experiences, because we're sure we'll fall short or fail in some way. With a fully formed defectiveness schema relentlessly stabbing you with its thorns of shame, insecurity, and depression, you cope in the only way that you thought possible—behind a heavy mask of crude design. A mask that you continue to wear to this day.

Our next story follows Monique and her experience with depression. As you read through her narrative, notice how the development of one defectiveness schema can look vastly different from another.

• Monique

Monique is a thirty-five-year-old woman who has been dealing with depression and alcohol abuse since she was twelve years old. In complete contrast to Lilly, Monique appears confident and witty upon approach. She actively seeks out novel interactions and is quick to speak her mind and offer her opinions, regardless of their content. She spends her days working as a camera girl for an adult entertainment website, and her evenings out on the town drinking at clubs and meeting her Tinder dates. Monique drinks, often to the point of unconsciousness, as without it she is unable to sleep through the night due to her racing thoughts and insomnia. Monique typically brings home the dates she meets online, especially if, in her words, "they can pull off the tough guy act." What this usually entails is a forceful, aggressive approach to both verbal and physical interactions. Monique usually never sees the same person more than twice, as she feels empowered whenever she takes the initiative to ghost or dump her partner after the second date.

Monique was a typical preteen in middle school when her emotional journey began. She grew up as a single child in an upper-middle-upper-class neighborhood with both her mother and her father, who were busy and hardworking individuals. Monique's early childhood was filled with exciting summers and large family gatherings. Since their house was spacious and had a large pool, it was often the gathering point of parties and family reunions. On one hot summer day, Monique's family was again playing host to the yearly family reunion. In attendance was her mother's youngest brother, Uncle Ray, who had started making regular appearances around the house after relocating for his new job. This had not been the most pleasant of developments for Monique due to the frequent discomfort she felt when he was around. When it came to Uncle Ray, Monique always felt the need to be on guard in his presence, as he had the tendency to sometimes brush up against her or give her a lingering stare, which would make her feel uncomfortable. Much to her surprise, the rest of the family seemed to think the world of Uncle Ray, always giving him shout-outs, laughs, and praise whenever he graced the group with his lewd jokes or aggressive remarks.

During this notably festive occasion, Monique was engaged in her usual routine of changing in the pool house before making her grand entrance cannonball. Just as she was finishing up, she heard a soft knock on the door, and Ray's voice called through the thin walls of the shack. "Hey, Monique, I think I left my watch on the sink. I'm coming in to get it." A cold shudder crawled down Monique's spine as she realized that in her haste, she had not locked the door. The moment she heard Ray open the door and then engage the lock behind him, Monique experienced the strangest feeling of leaving her body and then watching from afar as she was sexually traumatized. While only a minute or two had passed, for Monique it had seemed like a lifetime. The next time it happened, Monique was swimming alone after the conclusion of a family cookout, with all the other adults enjoying the second round of cocktails in the den. The last time was in the bathroom when Monique had woken up in the middle of the night. When the summer ended and the pool closed, Monique was broken.

One night, after enduring a family dinner at Uncle Ray's new house, Monique was able to muster up the courage to tell her parents about the numerous sexual assaults. The car ride was silent throughout the remainder of the thirty-minute-drive home. Feeling a mix of confusion and shame as she climbed the stairs to her room, she could faintly hear the sound of conflict between her mother and father. Curled into a fetal position under her covers, she heard her mother quietly open her door. "Sweetie, I know Uncle Ray can be a little crude and inappropriate at times, but he means well, and anything you think might have happened is probably just a little misinterpretation." She continued, "From now on, you don't need to spend any time with him if he's making you feel uncomfortable."

Monique's parents never brought up the topic again. They never forced Monique to be present at the dinner table or any pool party, and Ray was never invited to spend the weekends at their house—but they didn't take any action against Ray. Monique was never given the opportunity to receive treatment, and eventually she started to avoid all family gatherings.

Starting in high school, Monique chose to spend her time with a new group of friends who championed the title of Outcasts. She began to wear clothing that was often overexposing and frequently engaged in cutting behaviors to shut down the extreme emotions she felt. The abuse she experienced from her uncle and the abject lack of support and rejection from her parents left Monique with a profound sense that she was defective. And in time, her defectiveness schema took firm root in her psyche. I must have deserved the abuse, *Monique would often think.* My parents didn't do anything to protect me, so they must think I'm worthless. *Monique began engaging in casual sex with boys from her group and was often mistreated in her relationships. For Monique, it made sense when they would slap her around a bit. With each new partner, her thoughts would always bring her to the conclusion that she was broken and incapable of finding love. Eventually, she found that through the use of alcohol and drugs, she could further remove herself from the shame and depression of her schema. Sober, Monique was broken and unlovable, but with the help of alcohol, she learned how to numb her defectiveness pain.*

While contrasting significantly from Lilly's defectiveness presentation, Monique's self-destruction and careless abandon is no less an expression of depression. What characterizes your defectiveness schema? What thoughts and feelings similar to Lilly's and Monique's do you most often have?

How Defectiveness Feeds Your Depression

Picture for a moment the worst door-to-door solicitor you can imagine. This salesman comes knocking at your door on a daily basis to sell you the most horrible, negative thoughts you've ever imagined. Meet your defectiveness schema. It goes by one of those names that makes your stomach churn every time you hear it. It's already pounded at the door a few times today, but this time you can really hear the door shaking on its hinges when the schema announces its presence.

Your defectiveness schema says, "I know you've been trying to ignore me today, but I have a buy-one-get-one-free sale on *Nobody Is Ever Going to Love You!*" It continues, "You know that interview you have for a promotion tomorrow? Well, they're not planning on giving it to you; they know you're not as talented as your coworkers. They just pity you, because you have no friends, your family doesn't care about you, and your partner is just waiting for an excuse to leave!"

Your schema knows what to say in order to get you to buy the ideas that it's selling. Whether you decide to buy them, avoid them, or even attack them, it always finds a way to make those horrible, deep-seated thoughts come true. This is how your defectiveness schema feeds your depression, which can leave you sapped of energy, weighted down by self-criticism, and isolated from the world around you.

Of course, a defectiveness schema doesn't always show up as "typical" depression. It can also manifest in overwork, as you try to compensate for your inner feelings of defectiveness with outward success, or in aggression toward others rather than yourself, as you'll see in the next story.

• *Andre*

Andre is a forty-one-year-old, twice-divorced man who has devoted his life to his career as a master sergeant in the United States Marine Corps. Andre spends his days working relentlessly and usually long into the night. He pushes himself to extreme levels of exhaustion with twelve- to fourteen-hour workdays to fight the defective thoughts that plague him whenever he is idle. Andre does not have any close friends, just acquaintances. People will often go out of their way to avoid him, as Andre has developed a reputation for being quick to lash out whenever questions or problems are presented to him. Internally, Andre thinks little of himself. He often compares himself to others and concludes that every success or advantage he might have is only due to the fact that people do not know how truly defective and broken he is. In Andre's mind, it's only a matter of time before someone is able to see through his thinly veiled disguise. After all, his ex-wives and three children had seen through it; that's why they won't reach out to him anymore.

Andre has struggled with developing close relationships and feeling good about his own accomplishments for a long time. While he had never felt unloved by his parents, both his mother and his father were difficult to impress. As the eldest child in his family, he grew up feeling the pressure of setting the standard of excellence for his brother and sister, but his parents remained keen to pick out the faults and deficiencies that they saw whenever Andre sought out their praise. The one thing that always seemed to put them into a better mood was the two glasses of wine they enjoyed after a long day at work.

When Andre was fifteen years old, he was able to score his first job—a busboy clearing tables at one of the local wineries. He was more than excited with the prospect of surprising his parents with the accomplishment when he showed them his first paycheck. But on his second day on the job, as Andre was focused on clearing the aftermath of the Thursday-night crowd, he heard his father's voice among the remaining guests. After a few moments of eavesdropping, Andre came to the realization that his father had company with him, and that it was not his mother. Returning home later that night, Andre pulled his father aside and confronted him with the discovery. Later that night, Andre was awoken by a loud crashing noise that came from his parents' room. The sound was then accompanied by his mother's angry and accusatory screams, which his father returned in equal measure. Andre never saw his father again after that night. His parents separated after a long and bitter divorce. And Andre felt responsible—for the divorce, for the blame and rejection from his siblings for his father's physical absence, and for his mother's emotional withdrawal. The only conclusion that remained was that at his core, Andre was undeserving of the love and appreciation that he was denied.

The moment he was eligible to enlist, Andre joined the military, and he channeled his self-hatred into making himself as competent a marine as he could possibly be: an individual he believed could convince the world that he was stronger and ultimately superior to those around him. To an outsider, Andre might look like your prototypical tough marine. But on the inside, Andre was alone, depressed, and terrified that people would see him in the way that he saw himself—as wrong, defective, the reason bad things would happen. Andre found that his pain could be avoided through the relentless focus on work. Yet, in the end, like Lilly with her social avoidance and Monique with substances, Andre was a prisoner to his own defectiveness schema.

Conclusion

In this chapter, you've explored the concepts of schemas, defectiveness, and depression. You've learned how the development of these powerful scripts can influence our perceptions, behaviors, and relationships to such a degree that we remain trapped behind a mask of depression and suffering. Going through the stories of Lilly, Monique, and Andre, you've seen three different examples of how a defectiveness schema develops and takes hold of an individual's life. All three of the individuals look significantly different from each other, and each of them represents a different way of coping with the core beliefs that come with defectiveness, but in the end, all share the same core beliefs that they're defective: unworthy in some deep way.

The concepts we've discussed in this first chapter will be reviewed throughout the book, as you begin to explore how your own defectiveness schema developed and how it has taken your life hostage. In the next chapter, we will be guiding you through a process of assessment that will help you explore the context for your defectiveness schema and develop a deeper understanding of its power.

Chapter 2

Assessment

Now that you've begun your journey toward learning more about your defectiveness schema and how it relates to depression, this chapter will guide you through the process of looking more closely at the parts of your life that may have contributed to and impacted your symptoms of depression: your family life, your social life, your career, your engagement with your community, and more. For instance, you might find that your negative beliefs show up in the exchanges you have within your family, the ways in which you navigate your relationships, the connection you have with your career, and how you interact with the various communities in your environment. Several assessment measures are used to help uncover the presence of a defectiveness schema—to explore the intensity of depression you may feel in your life, and to help uncover more about your values, the things that matter to you, which can help motivate change. In this chapter, we'll guide you through those measures. And by the time you're done, you'll have both a better sense of your current situation and a way to measure the progress you've made as you work to change it.

1. Defectiveness Schema Questionnaire

2. Valued Living Questionnaire, Parts 1 and 2

3. Acceptance and Action Questionnaire 2

4. Automatic Thoughts Questionnaire

5. The CES Depression Scale

Defectiveness Schema Questionnaire

The first assessment we will explore in this chapter pertains directly to the thoughts and feelings that are characteristic of your defectiveness schema. Read through the statements below, and circle *T* or *F* according to whether you think the statement is mostly true or mostly false. In cases where it's a close decision, go with your first impulse. Make sure to mark the rating that is closest to how you emotionally feel, rather than what you logically think is verifiably true. It's important to complete every item, marking either *T* or *F* (but not both), in order to get an accurate score at the end.

Statement	True	False
1. I am worthy of love and respect.	T	F
2. I often feel flawed or defective.	T	F
3. I feel okay about myself.	T	F
4. Nobody I desire would desire me if they really got to know me.	T	F
5. I have legitimate needs I deserve to fill.	T	F
6. I'm dull and boring and can't make interesting conversation.	T	F
7. I count for something in the world.	T	F
8. I'm unattractive.	T	F
9. People I like and respect often like and respect me.	T	F
10. I don't deserve much attention or respect.	T	F

Once you've completed the assessment, it's time to score it. Look at your answers for items 1, 3, 5, 7, and 9. For each *F* you marked off, give yourself one point. Then, look at your answers for items 2, 4, 6, 8, and 10. For each *T* you marked off, give yourself one point. Then, total your scores. The number you get indicates how much you agree with the statement "I'm defective, inferior, and unlovable."

Let's look at the questionnaire filled out by Andre from the last chapter.

1.	I am worthy of love and respect.	T	(F)
2.	I often feel flawed or defective.	(T)	F
3.	I feel okay about myself.	T	(F)
4.	Nobody I desire would desire me if they really got to know me.	(T)	F
5.	I have legitimate needs I deserve to fill.	(T)	F
6.	I'm dull and boring and can't make interesting conversation.	(T)	F
7.	I count for something in the world.	(T)	F
8.	I'm unattractive.	(T)	F
9.	People I like and respect often like and respect me.	T	(F)
10.	I don't deserve much attention or respect.	(T)	F

Andre got a score of 8, indicating he identifies strongly with the statement "I'm defective, inferior, and unlovable." And as you can see from the particular items he marked as true or false, the self-blame he internalized during his parents' divorce has remained consistent even into his adult life and developed into an overall sense of unworthiness. He continues to battle with this on a daily basis, keeping him far removed from the close interpersonal relationships that would contest his sense of defectiveness.

Valued Living Questionnaire, Parts 1 and 2

This next assessment measure, the Valued Living Questionnaire, will help you get a better idea of how well you have been living your life in accordance with your values—the things that matter to you, the qualities you really want to exemplify throughout your life—and your priorities. In the first part of this assessment, we want you to rate the importance of different life areas on a scale of 1 to 10, with 1 being not at all important and 10 being extremely important. The purpose of highlighting the different aspects of your life that you deem important will be coming into play as a critical aspect of your journey to wellness. As the healthy replacement to the behaviors that fuel your depression, the values you highlight in this section will become your guiding light in the darkness. They will serve as the motivation for your positive transformation and give you a reason to move into the uncharted waters of change.

In the second part of this assessment, we want you to indicate how consistently you have adhered to the listed values throughout the past week. The point of this exercise is to see the relationship between the areas of your life that you value as important and how successful you've been in acting upon the importance you ascribe to these valued areas. As an example, if you rate the domain of "marriage, couples, intimate relations" as a 9 or 10, but you rate your consistency with that domain as a 4 or 5, we want you to start thinking about why that differential exists. With it being such an important domain in your life, what is the cause of it being so poorly put into practice? As we start to explore the nature of values within this treatment, these are the questions we will help you both clarify and answer. Please complete the following parts 1 and 2 of the Valued Living Questionnaire on the following two pages.

Valued Living Questionnaire: Self-Care Assessment Part 1
(Wilson et al., 2010)

Below are areas of life that are valued by some people. This questionnaire will help clarify your own quality of life in each of these areas. One aspect of quality of life involves the importance you put on different areas of living. Rate the importance of each area (by circling a number) on a scale of 1 to 10. A 1 means that area is *not at all important*. A 10 means that area is *extremely important*. Not everyone will value all of these areas or value all areas the same. Rate each area according to *your own personal sense of importance*. At the end is a place for you to reflect on your responses.

Area	not at all important						extremely important			
Family (other than marriage or parenting)	1	2	3	4	5	6	7	8	9	10
Marriage, couples, intimate relationships	1	2	3	4	5	6	7	8	9	10
Parenting	1	2	3	4	5	6	7	8	9	10
Friends and social life	1	2	3	4	5	6	7	8	9	10
Work	1	2	3	4	5	6	7	8	9	10
Education and training	1	2	3	4	5	6	7	8	9	10
Recreation and fun	1	2	3	4	5	6	7	8	9	10
Spirituality, meaning, and purpose in life	1	2	3	4	5	6	7	8	9	10
Citizenship and community life	1	2	3	4	5	6	7	8	9	10
Physical self-care (nutrition, exercise, rest, and sleep)	1	2	3	4	5	6	7	8	9	10

Reflection: How do you feel about this? Are there any areas that surprised you?

_____

_____

_____

Valued Living Questionnaire: Self-Care Assessment Part 2
(Wilson et al., 2010)

In this section, please give a rating of how *consistent* your actions have been with each of your values. Please note that this is *not* asking about your ideal in each area *or* what others think of you. Everyone does better in some areas than in others. People also do better at some times than at others. *Please just indicate how you think you have been doing during the past week.* Rate each area (by circling a number) on a scale of 1 to 10. A 1 means that your actions have been *completely inconsistent with your value.* A 10 means that your actions have been *completely consistent with your value.*

During the past week, how consistent have you been with your values?

Area	completely inconsistent					completely consistent				
Family (other than marriage or parenting)	1	2	3	4	5	6	7	8	9	10
Marriage, couples, intimate relationships	1	2	3	4	5	6	7	8	9	10
Parenting	1	2	3	4	5	6	7	8	9	10
Friends and social life	1	2	3	4	5	6	7	8	9	10
Work	1	2	3	4	5	6	7	8	9	10
Education and training	1	2	3	4	5	6	7	8	9	10
Recreation and fun	1	2	3	4	5	6	7	8	9	10
Spirituality, meaning, and purpose in life	1	2	3	4	5	6	7	8	9	10
Citizenship and community life	1	2	3	4	5	6	7	8	9	10
Physical self-care (nutrition, exercise, rest, and sleep)	1	2	3	4	5	6	7	8	9	10

Total: _____

Add up the total circled numbers for part 2, where 10 is the minimum and 100 is the maximum. The higher the number, the more likely you are to experience happiness in your life.

Acceptance and Action Questionnaire 2

Our third measure that we'll be using to assess and chart your progress is the Assessment and Action Questionnaire 2 (or AAQ-2). One of the more fundamental aspects of this journey you have started on is learning to develop and embrace a level of psychological flexibility. This is the degree to which you are able to resist getting caught in the torrent of emotions, impulses, and thoughts that might come up in a given situation. Instead of being overwhelmed by the tide and responding in the short term (which might give in-the-moment relief), you are able to step back and use your core values to dictate your behavior.

What does it mean to be psychologically *inflexible*? Imagine yourself walking in a circle that is so well traveled that it has become a trench that now stands several feet deep. This trench is the result of you responding to your environment in ways that might have once made sense or provided relief, but only for the immediacy. You've been responding the same way to problems and barriers for as long as you can remember, so much so that you're not even sure what it might look like to peek over the trench walls and approach things differently. Psychological flexibility, by contrast, is the ability to fully be in the present moment, even if what you're facing is uncomfortable, and behave in ways that serve your values, the things that really matter to you.

One of the primary goals of this workbook is to help you learn how to crawl out of the rigid thought traps that have worked to keep you as stuck and depressed as you have been. This is where the AAQ-2 comes in: to help you get a better understanding of where you stand with regard to your level of psychological flexibility and how deep of a trench you might be circling. Complete the AAQ-2 by marking how true the following statements are to you, on a scale of 1 to 7 (1 being *never true* and 7 being *always true*).

Acceptance and Action Questionnaire 2 (AAQ-2)
(Bond et al., 2011)

Below you will find a list of statements. Please rate how true each statement is for you by circling a number next to it. Use the scale below to make your choice.

1	2	3	4	5	6	7
Never true	Very seldom true	Seldom true	Sometimes true	Frequently true	Almost always true	Always true

1. My painful experiences and memories make it difficult for me to live a life that I would value.	1	2	3	4	5	6	7
2. I'm afraid of my feelings.	1	2	3	4	5	6	7
3. I worry about not being able to control my worries and feelings.	1	2	3	4	5	6	7
4. My painful memories prevent me from having a fulfilling life.	1	2	3	4	5	6	7
5. Emotions cause problems in my life.	1	2	3	4	5	6	7
6. It seems like most people are handling their lives better than I am.	1	2	3	4	5	6	7
7. Worries get in the way of my success.	1	2	3	4	5	6	7

Total: _____

Let's review your scores and see how things turned out. An average score on the AAQ-2 is 18.51 in the general population, with a score greater than 24 characterizing a life experience that is most likely quite distressful and overwhelming, with a notably high trench wall. Remember Monique's experience with depression and defectiveness? She rated a score of

38 on the AAQ-2, demonstrating that she is really struggling to climb out of the trench her defectiveness has created for her. Not only is she haunted by her experiences and memories to such a degree that she is constantly shutting them out or numbing them with alcohol, but she also spends the majority of her life trying to find ways to escape from the trench without realizing that she continues to reinforce it and dig herself deeper. Now, if you're looking at your score and feeling concerned that you scored above a 24 (or even above Monique), take into consideration that you've already taken steps to stop the reinforcement of your trench by picking up this guide and looking for another option in contrast to those who continue down their narrow path until their time runs out. Realizing that you've been walking in circles can be one of the most difficult steps to achieve, and if you're reading this, you're already starting to challenge the walls that hold you prisoner.

Automatic Thoughts Questionnaire

So far we've assessed your defectiveness schema, taken a snapshot of your values, and marked the starting point for your psychological flexibility. With this next assessment, we will be looking at how frequently your depressive symptoms have been hounding you with negative thoughts and to what degree you believe them. Remember that evil salesman we discussed in chapter 1—your defectiveness schema? This is the part of the assessment where you can take a close look at what thoughts it's been selling you and how often you've been buying them. Your depression is able to maintain its control over your behaviors and interactions by constantly convincing you that you're worthless and powerless, and that nothing you do will make any change to that effect. When you complete the Automatic Thoughts Questionnaire (ATQ), you are going to get a good understanding as to how malicious your solicitor has been over the years! Like the other measures you have completed thus far, the ATQ will present you with a list of statements that you will rate in terms of both frequency (how often this thought has occurred to you over the last week) and degree of belief (how much you believe this thought when you have it). The rating for the ATQ is on a 1-to-5 scale: with 1 being *not at all* and 5 being *all the time* when it comes to frequency, and 1 being *not at all* and 5 being *totally* when it comes to degree of belief. Please complete the ATQ and add up your scores into two data points on the right and left side of the assessment (one total score for degree of belief, and one for frequency).

Automatic Thoughts Questionnaire (ATQ)
(Hollon & Kendall, 1980)

Listed below are a variety of thoughts that pop into people's heads. Please read each thought and indicate how frequently, if at all, the thought occurred to you over the last week. Please read each item carefully and circle the appropriate answers on the answer sheet in the following fashion 1 = *not at all*, 2 = *sometimes*, 3 = *moderately often*, 4 = *often*, and 5 = *all the time*. Then, please indicate how strongly, if at all, you tend to believe that thought, when it occurs. On the right-hand side of the page, circle the appropriate answers in the following fashion 1 = *not at all*, 2 = *somewhat*, 3 = *moderately*, 4 = *very much*, and 5 = *totally*.

Items	Frequency	Degree of Belief
1. I feel like I'm up against the world.	1 2 3 4 5	1 2 3 4 5
2. I'm no good.	1 2 3 4 5	1 2 3 4 5
3. Why can't I ever succeed?	1 2 3 4 5	1 2 3 4 5
4. No one understands me.	1 2 3 4 5	1 2 3 4 5
5. I've let people down.	1 2 3 4 5	1 2 3 4 5
6. I don't think I can go on.	1 2 3 4 5	1 2 3 4 5
7. I wish I were a better person.	1 2 3 4 5	1 2 3 4 5
8. I'm so weak.	1 2 3 4 5	1 2 3 4 5
9. My life's not going the way I want it to.	1 2 3 4 5	1 2 3 4 5
10. I'm so disappointed in myself.	1 2 3 4 5	1 2 3 4 5
11. Nothing feels good anymore.	1 2 3 4 5	1 2 3 4 5
12. I can't stand this anymore.	1 2 3 4 5	1 2 3 4 5

13. I can't get started.	1 2 3 4 5	1 2 3 4 5
14. What's wrong with me?	1 2 3 4 5	1 2 3 4 5
15. I wish I were somewhere else.	1 2 3 4 5	1 2 3 4 5
16. I can't get things together.	1 2 3 4 5	1 2 3 4 5
17. I hate myself.	1 2 3 4 5	1 2 3 4 5
18. I'm worthless.	1 2 3 4 5	1 2 3 4 5
19. I wish I could just disappear.	1 2 3 4 5	1 2 3 4 5
20. What's the matter with me?	1 2 3 4 5	1 2 3 4 5
21. I'm a loser.	1 2 3 4 5	1 2 3 4 5
22. My life is a mess.	1 2 3 4 5	1 2 3 4 5
23. I'm a failure.	1 2 3 4 5	1 2 3 4 5
24. I'll never make it.	1 2 3 4 5	1 2 3 4 5
25. I feel so helpless.	1 2 3 4 5	1 2 3 4 5
26. Something has to change.	1 2 3 4 5	1 2 3 4 5
27. There must be something wrong with me.	1 2 3 4 5	1 2 3 4 5
28. My future is bleak.	1 2 3 4 5	1 2 3 4 5
29. It's just not worth it.	1 2 3 4 5	1 2 3 4 5
30. I can't finish anything.	1 2 3 4 5	1 2 3 4 5

Total: _____

How did you score on this measure? For reference, individuals who don't suffer with depression typically score in the upper 30s to 50s. People with depression tend to score in the upper 80s to 100s. For instance, Lilly, who struggled with her grades and the emotional neglect from her mother, scored a 105 on her degrees of belief and a 102 on her frequency of negative automatic thoughts.

The negative automatic thoughts you receive from your defectiveness schema on a daily basis have played a major role in keeping you stuck in the cycle of self-criticism, avoidance, and depression. As you continue forward in this journey toward wellness, you will learn how to respond differently to your solicitor, so that the constant barrage of negative thoughts becomes a manageable choice that no longer keeps you from being the person you want to be.

The CES Depression Scale

The CES Depression Scale (CES-D) is your final step through this chapter of self-report and introspection. Developed by the Center for Epidemiologic Studies, part of the National Institute of Mental Health, it is a thorough measure of mood. In the worksheet, complete all the prompts, add up your score, and use the interpretation key at the end to see where you fall on the spectrum.

The CES Depression Scale (CES-D)

Using the scale below, indicate the number that best describes how often you felt or behaved this way *during the past week.*

0 = rarely or none of the time (less than 1 day)

1 = some or a little of the time (1–2 days)

2 = occasionally or a moderate amount of the time (3–4 days)

3 = most or all of the time (5–7 days)

During the past week:

1. I was bothered by things that don't usually bother me.	
2. I did not feel like eating; my appetite was poor.	
3. I felt I couldn't shake off the blues, even with help from my family or friends.	
4. I felt that I was just as good as other people.	
5. I had trouble keeping my mind on what I was doing.	
6. I felt depressed.	
7. I felt that everything I did was an effort.	
8. I felt hopeful about the future.	
9. I thought my life had been a failure.	
10. I felt fearful.	
11. My sleep was restless.	
12. I was happy.	
13. I talked less than usual.	
14. I felt lonely.	
15. People were unfriendly.	
16. I enjoyed life.	
17. I had crying spells.	
18. I felt sad.	
19. I felt that people disliked me.	
20. I could not get going.	
Total: _____	

You can score the CES-D by *reverse-scoring* items 4, 8, 12, and 16—meaning, if your response to item 4 was "some or a little of the time," rather than giving yourself a 1, you'd give yourself a 2—and then adding up your scores for all the items. Scores will range anywhere from 0 to 60, with higher scores indicating a higher level of depression. The average score for the general population is 8. People with depression tend to score 24 or higher.

The CES-D is also sensitive to changes in your mood, so it's a good way to measure improvement as you work your way through this treatment program. You are encouraged to take the CES-D at least three times—at the beginning, midpoint, and end—to gauge your response to the program. You can keep a record of your scores in the spaces below:

Date: _____   Score: _____

Date: _____   Score: _____

Date: _____   Score: _____

Date: _____   Score: _____

As for Lilly, Monique, and Andre, all three scored high enough to indicate a level of depression that was significant enough to cause daily impairment within their lives. Lilly's score of 28 characterized a moderate level of depression, which shows that her symptoms are likely present more often than not, and affect her both physically (feeling exhausted, losing weight) and mentally (negative thoughts about herself). Monique's score of 33 shows that she is suffering from severe depressive symptoms, which are likely always impacting her to some degree, and which persist on both a physical and a mental level with debilitating effect. Finally, Andre's score of 20 exemplifies borderline clinical depression, which might present as symptoms either internally or externally, but not to the degree of impairment that would lead to significant deviations from his daily routine. How did your scores compare with the others?

Conclusion

Congratulations, you have made it through the final assessment for this chapter. It's not an easy task to complete all the intrusive assessments we challenged you with in this chapter. Many of the questions presented in these measures might have kicked up painful memories of the past or served as a gross reminder to the pain that you experience with your depression. Give yourself some compassion and acknowledgment for drawing your starting point in the sand and looking at what might be the painful realities that you cope with day to day. By completing this chapter, you have not only started to touch upon the lessons to come, but also you will be able to see just how far you've grown at the journey's end. Once you've read through all of the chapters and completed all of the exercises, test yourself again on these measurements. As you begin to practice the exercises and use the tools we give you, you will learn to improve the consistency of your values, boost your psychological flexibility, change your relationship toward negative thoughts, and slowly lift the mask of your depression.

Chapter 3

Defectiveness Coping Behaviors

In the last chapter, we guided you through the five assessments highlighting important areas of functioning that are likely being impacted by your depression and defectiveness schema. In this chapter, we are going to explore different ways in which your defectiveness schema can guide your behavior. Back in chapter 1, we discussed how your defectiveness schema can change the lens through which you view yourself, others, and the world. Delving into the history of Lilly, Monique, and Andre (all of whom were battling with defectiveness), you saw how each responded to their schema in noticeably different ways. Your defectiveness schema likely developed from experiences you had early in life. It might not have been a singular traumatic event but a repetition of interactions that constructed your negative core beliefs. You have gone through your life with your own unique way of coping with the unwanted thoughts, memories, and emotions that get triggered by your schema. In your attempt to silence these thoughts and feelings that make you feel self-conscious, depressed, or alone, you have engaged in behaviors that provide temporary relief from the pain, though they ultimately reinforce your defectiveness schema. This chapter will outline these various defectiveness coping behaviors (DCBs).

You wouldn't have used these DCBs early on if they were not effective. By helping you tolerate a traumatic experience or cope with a difficult childhood, you learned that by relying on these behaviors, you could respond to your schema pain in a way that made it more tolerable. This might have taken several forms, such as socially disconnecting from the world, dominating individuals who threatened to expose you, or surrendering in your interactions so as to not experience the pain of conflict. Below we have outlined the ten common defectiveness coping behaviors that were first described by Jeffrey Young (Young et al., 2003), which are grouped into three major types: overcompensation, surrender, and avoidance. As you read through the following behaviors, consider which ones seem applicable to you. Which behavior (or behaviors) do you find yourself using in response to a defectiveness-triggering event?

Ten Common Defectiveness Coping Behaviors

- Overcompensation

    - *Aggression or hostility:* You counterattack by blaming, criticizing, challenging, or being resistant.

    - *Dominance or excessive self-assertion:* You try to control others in order to accomplish your goals.

    - *Recognition seeking or status seeking:* You overcompensate by trying to impress others and get attention through high achievement and status.

    - *Manipulation and exploitation:* You meet your own needs without letting others know what you're doing. This may involve the use of seduction or not being completely truthful with others.

    - *Passive-aggressiveness or rebellion:* You appear to be compliant but will rebel by procrastinating, complaining, being tardy, pouting, or performing poorly.

- Surrender

    - *Compliance or dependence:* You rely on others, give in, become dependent, behave passively, avoid conflict, and try to please others.

- Avoidance

    - *Social withdrawal or excessive autonomy:* You isolate yourself socially, disconnect, and withdraw from others. You may appear to be excessively independent and self-reliant, or you may engage in solitary activities, such as reading, watching television, computer use, or solitary work.

- *Compulsive stimulation seeking:* You seek excitement or distraction through compulsive shopping, sex, gambling, risk taking, or physical activity.

- *Addictive self-soothing:* You seek excitement with drugs, alcohol, food, or excessive self-stimulation.

- *Psychological withdrawal:* You escape through dissociation, denial, fantasy, or other internal forms of withdrawal.

Maybe you don't just use one coping behavior. Perhaps you use a few of them that were described in the list, depending on the situation that you find yourself in. For instance, you might engage in overcompensation through recognition or status seeking in a work or academic setting, constantly trying to impress or succeed in order to silence your fear of being seen as an imposter. You might surrender in your personal relationships, engaging in them with a passive dependence, such that you are constantly trying to please those who do not reciprocate. Finally, you might be practicing the avoidant style in a variety of your daily activities, such as excessive drinking, compulsive shopping, or evading interpersonal interactions. As you begin to identify the DCBs that have made themselves commonplace in your relationships, you will begin to move toward the stage of developing a deeper awareness of when these behaviors present themselves and the impact they have throughout the domains of your life.

This process of awareness starts by first looking at the situations in which you find yourself engaging in the behaviors that have been described above. Your schema can be triggered in any of the six relationship domains: work, friendship, family, partner, parenting, or community. Think back to a difficult or troubling interaction that played out in a domain that you consider important, an interaction that left you feeling vulnerable, depressed, or angry—emotions or thoughts that were most likely stimulated by your defectiveness schema. And then see if you used one of the ten DCBs previously described.

With this situation you have in mind: In which relationship domain is this taking place?

_____

By highlighting the type of relationship, you are adding to an important part of the puzzle. Developing awareness for the domains in which you have specific triggers will help you reveal patterns that will become pivotal in the change process.

Moving toward the next part of the crime scene, we want you think back to what thoughts were occurring at the time. Thoughts are your in-the-moment appraisals of a situation. They might sound like *I knew they didn't love me*, or *I don't deserve to be happy*. They're an essential piece of evidence in that they often communicate your schema-related fears.

Quickly jot down the thoughts you had in the situation you're thinking about.

_____

_____

_____

Next, we step deeper into the crime scene to look at what emotions you were experiencing in the moment. Emotions such as anger, fear, sadness, or irritability can give you a temperature to color the internal sensations that were occurring as the situation unfolded.

Which emotions did you experience in the situation you're thinking about?

_____

_____

_____

Finally, we arrive at the behavioral reaction or outcome of the event. This is when you look back at that list of DCBs and see whether your reaction was characteristic of overcompensation, surrender, or avoidance. Now, perhaps you didn't respond with a DCB, but instead just had an urge to do so. You want to capture this as well, because it will provide you with more important evidence that you will use in the process moving forward.

In the situation you're thinking about, what urges did you feel? How did you act in response?

_____

_____

_____

This is the basic process that will help you uncover the influence your defectiveness schema has on your behavior. Consider the situations that leave you with a sense of defectiveness and exacerbate your depression, and carefully unpack the thoughts you had, the way you felt, and the behaviors you used in response (or the urges you felt, if you didn't react). Over time, you'll gain a better sense of what tends to trigger your defectiveness and the characteristic pattern of your behavior in response, which often will feed your depression.

What follows is a worksheet that will help you track what we'll call your defectiveness triggers. Below is an example of a worksheet completed by Lilly, whose story of defectiveness was explored in chapter 1.

Defectiveness Triggers Worksheet

Domain	(Work) Friendship Family Partner Parenting Community
Situation	I overhear that a few of my coworkers are going to be meeting later for dinner and drinks. Nobody has approached me to see if I would want to join them.
Thoughts	I'm not a part of the group. My coworkers don't like or respect me. My coworkers think something is wrong with me.
Emotions	Irritation, sadness, anger.
Urges (if you didn't react)	Hide away from the people who don't respect or care about me. Avoid socializing with people.
Behavioral reactions	I hide out in my little corner of the office and avoid any and all interactions with my coworkers for the rest of the week.

Looking at how Lilly completed her worksheet, let's break down each part of this equation. First, Lilly's defectiveness schema was triggered in the domain of work, when she overheard her coworkers discussing plans to meet for dinner, to which she had yet to be invited. The lack of an invite caused Lilly to think that her coworkers did not respect her or thought something was wrong with her. This prompted her to experience the emotions of irritation and sadness, feeling left out and rejected from the milieu. In response to these difficult thoughts and emotions, Lilly spent the rest of the week hiding away from her coworkers, avoiding any social interactions. Feeling the full weight of her defectiveness schema, Lilly's DCB of avoidance kicked into high gear, driving her to avoid her peers as much as possible so as to mitigate any further pain she would feel from the depression.

As you can probably imagine, Lilly was not invited to the dinner. Rather than making herself appear open and available to socialize, Lilly avoided any interactions with her peers. By avoiding her peers, two things occurred at once. Lilly was able to avoid further defectiveness pain, but she also reinforced her perception that she was disliked at the office. It is possible that Lilly's perception was accurate, but it is also possible that there were other reasons why her coworkers had not invited her out. They might have just started planning the event and had yet to approach Lilly, but they did intend to do so. The dinner plans might also have been limited to just two or three individuals, with no negative impression toward Lilly in the first place. The coworkers might have also perceived that Lilly would not have wanted to attend the dinner; to avoid the anticipated rejection, they only approached people who seemed interested and available. In the end, irrespective of the actual motives of her coworkers, Lilly's avoidance behaviors ensured that she would be left alone.

Now that you have reviewed the steps and seen an example of what a completed Defectiveness Triggers Worksheet looks like, fill one out yourself. (This worksheet is also available for download at http://www.newharbinger.com/45540.)

Defectiveness Triggers Worksheet

Domain	Work Friendship Family Partner Parenting Community
Situation	
Thoughts	
Emotions	
Urges (if you didn't react)	
Behavioral reactions	

Now that you've completed the Defectiveness Triggers Worksheet, it's important for you to start looking at what impact your DCBs are having on the domains of your life. In Lilly's case, her DCB of avoidance served to isolate her from her peers and remove any opportunities she might have had to develop closer relationships with her coworkers. When you follow the urge to engage in the DCB, you reduce your pain in the moment, but this ensures that your defectiveness remains unchallenged. When you don't bring the entire chain of events into awareness, it is pretty easy to see how the DCBs and their consequences can continue to play out. Since it is easy to positively associate avoidance of certain situations with the avoidance of emotional pain, in the same way that we do with physical pain, DCBs can seem like a clear win in the way that they can lessen the experience of suffering in the short term. What is more difficult to see, however, is how using DCBs will keep you stuck in a cycle of depression, doomed to continue sacrificing what you value in life for temporary relief in the moment.

The next exercise will ask you to start capturing the consequences of your engagement in DCBs. Like the Defectiveness Triggers Worksheet, the DCB Consequence Worksheet will have you record a situation where your defectiveness schema was triggered. Complete the worksheet by first documenting the thoughts, emotions, and behavioral reactions that resulted from the situation. Lastly, record what the consequence of your behavior was. Below is an example of the DCB Consequence Worksheet completed by Andre, whose history was explored in chapter 1.

Andre responded to his defectiveness schema with overcompensation, using passive-aggression and manipulation to feel better when he felt that his potential partner was losing interest. In the moment, he felt that he had gained the upper hand and was no longer vulnerable to his depressive thoughts. However, the resulting consequences of his DCB were that any further connection with his romantic interest had been destroyed. Ultimately, Andre's behavior reinforced his defectiveness schema. Following Andre's example, complete your own DCB Consequence Worksheet below. (This worksheet is also available for download at http://www.newharbinger.com/45540.)

DCB Consequence Worksheet

Domain	Work Friendship Family (Partner) Parenting Community
Situation	My date tells me that she needs to cancel our upcoming dinner plans due to a scheduling conflict.
Thoughts	She's lying to me. She's not really interested in me. I must have said something that showed her I was broken.
Emotions	Anger, frustration, sadness.
Behavioral reactions	Be passive-aggressive with my communication. Shut her down when she tries to reschedule our date. Lie to her and try to hook up with someone else.
Consequences	She stops responding to my calls and texts.

DCB Consequence Worksheet

Domain	Work Friendship Family Partner Parenting Community
Situation	
Thoughts	
Emotions	
Behavioral reactions	
Consequences	

At this point in your journey, you have been given tools to help you uncover the problem. Now that you have a better understanding of defectiveness coping behaviors and have completed the exercises provided in this chapter, continue to use the worksheets over the next eight weeks, and you'll begin to understand the cycle of your own personal defectiveness schema. This type of awareness is a fundamental part of the change process. You'll need to be diligent in completing the worksheets provided in this chapter, and to do so multiple times (it is best to fill out two or more worksheets every week), in order to capture the full spectrum of your defectiveness coping behavior. (Blank worksheets can be found online at http://www .newharbinger.com/45540.)

Once you have a sense of how your DCBs operate and the consequences they have in your life, you can begin to break the cycle. Moving forward, you will continue to explore the costs of your DCBs along with the concept of accepting painful experiences that you cannot change, and how you can choose to respond differently to your defectiveness schema.

Chapter 4

From Avoidance to Acceptance

If you think back, that feeling of defectiveness has been with you a long time. Chances are that it was with you in high school, and perhaps much earlier. Over all these years, it has been triggered hundreds, even thousands of times. No matter how much success you've had, how many friends care for you, how well your career has gone, or how loved you are by your family, the feeling persists and seems impervious to all the positive experiences in your life. Your fear, shame, and sadness are intense; your DCBs may feel like the only ways you can deal with them. But—what if there were a different way to respond?

• *Raul and Arielle*

Take, for example, Raul's experiences. He's a manager of a bank branch and lives in a pleasant suburb, his house overlooking a tree-ringed lake. His wife is a speech therapist who loves her job and her family (they have two sons in grade school). Raul volunteers for his local fire department, as well as for progressive causes. He is well regarded in his community as someone who's successful and civic-minded. None of this, including his luxurious new car, has changed Raul's basic feeling about himself. His defectiveness schema is triggered by even slight criticism, small mistakes, forgetting something, and the suggestion that he knows less about certain things than he should.

Every time Raul's defectiveness feelings are activated, he gets angry. Sometimes he expresses irritation openly; sometimes he holds it in and shuts down. His subordinates at the bank, and at home, his wife and boys, are often targets as he copes with surges of shame and self-disgust. He ruminates about mistakes and small failures, and these self-judgments have precipitated chronic depression.

No matter how Raul tries to suppress or drive away his sense of defectiveness, it's always there, waiting to leap up. He can trace it back to childhood, when his dad—ever angry and dissatisfied with life—would mock him for being afraid of things. "Oh, little Raul doesn't like the water; he's afraid to get wet." "Are you afraid of the ball, Raul? Catch the damn ball!" "Raul's upset 'cause somebody made fun of him. Just give the kid a good sock—but you're afraid of that, too, aren't you?" From then on, criticism from anyone evoked the same shame and sadness, the same painful conviction that he was less than other people.

Arielle had a different background. As long as she could remember, she'd always been shy. She thought of herself as awkward and clumsy and assumed everybody saw her the same way. In middle school she somehow got included in a group of smart girls, but she rarely could think of anything interesting to say. She happily went along with whatever the group did, including things she actually knew were wrong. They once had a scrape with the police when they posted untrue accusations about a teacher they despised on the internet.

Despite good grades and making the tennis team (with a low rank, she remembers), Arielle continued to feel like a "blatant loser." Her parents, who were supportive, encouraged Arielle to join the poetry club at school, but she spent most of her after-school time in her room, never showing her writing to anyone. They later encouraged her to apply to a well-regarded college, but she went to a community college, saying "it's better that way." What she meant was that she felt safer by withdrawing from challenges because her sense of worthlessness and shame were too painful when triggered.

Now a teller at Raul's bank, she thinks of things she wishes she'd done, struggles with depression, and spends a lot of time watching television in her small apartment. Arielle's defectiveness schema has effectively paralyzed her, and even now it keeps her from using her talents.

There's a reason why the defectiveness belief is so enduring. Like all schemas, it's a way to organize, sort, and remember our experiences. Raul has a big basket labeled "less than," in which he puts all his past mistakes and failures. There is no corresponding memory basket to hold his many successes, so when he thinks about himself, all that comes up are memories from the "less than" basket. Similarly, Arielle, shy and believing people see her as *awkward and uninteresting, has a "blatant loser" basket that holds every awkward moment, every time she couldn't think of something clever to say.*

You can begin to see, now, why that old defectiveness belief is so strong—it's a basket of bad memories that you forever dip into when thinking about yourself. And every one of those memories, now forged into an amalgam of negative self-regard, triggers those familiar and painful defectiveness-driven feelings: fear, shame, and sadness.

DCBs Have Made the Pain Worse

In chapter 3, you examined the negative consequences of your defectiveness coping behaviors (DCBs). If you looked at your DCBs carefully and were honest with yourself, you probably discovered two things:

- Despite all these years of trying to cope with and mute the pain associated with your defectiveness schema, the pain is still there. The shame, the sense of wrongness, and the sad, negative feelings about yourself are just one triggering event away. Not only is the pain still there, but so is the schema—worse if anything, because you've collected so many negative memories in your basket.

- What's more, there are new forms of pain shaped by your DCBs. The fear, shame, and sadness are still there. And because you've used DCBs—anger, withdrawal, or surrender—new problems have arisen in your life.

Think about a time when you used a DCB in response to your fear, shame, or sadness. What were the consequences?

_____

_____

_____

_____

Odds are that new pain arose. You may feel more alone because anger and withdrawal are hard on people, and some have pulled away from you. You may feel that you've lost control of your life because you avoid challenges or always give in (surrender) to what other people want. You may now feel anxiety because you expect to be rejected (for your defectiveness) and live constantly on guard for such a hurt. Your sadness may have deepened into a chronic state, or your shame into a caustic self-hate. The DCBs, well intended as they may be, have backfired and only provided more evidence for your defectiveness beliefs.

On the following checklist, check off the kinds of pain associated with (1) your defectiveness schema and (2) the outcomes from DCBs.

Defectiveness Outcomes Checklist

Defectiveness: Emotional Outcomes

- ☐ Fear of disapproval
- ☐ Fear of being exposed
- ☐ Shame
- ☐ Sense of being unworthy, less than
- ☐ Sense of failure
- ☐ Feelings of sadness
- ☐ Fear of challenges
- ☐ Anger and defensiveness

Defectiveness: Coping Behavior Outcomes (enduring consequences of using DCBs over time)

- ☐ Aloneness
- ☐ Shyness or social withdrawal
- ☐ Feeling helpless or controlled by others
- ☐ Chronic depression
- ☐ Self-hate or self-disgust
- ☐ Problems in relationships
- ☐ Loss of friendships
- ☐ Conflict with romantic partner
- ☐ Loss of jobs
- ☐ Feeling stuck at work, unable to advance
- ☐ Unable to express your feelings and needs
- ☐ Feeling of missing out on your potential
- ☐ Feeling numb
- ☐ Excessive self-soothing or pleasure seeking
- ☐ Excessive use of drugs or alcohol
- ☐ Internet or other addictions
- ☐ Overworking
- ☐ Perfectionism

As you already know, the emotional pain associated with your defectiveness schema is considerable. But the pain that's a consequence of using DCBs is often far worse. Trying to avoid the defectiveness pain can move you out of the frying pan and into the fire. The Defectiveness Outcomes Checklist may have demonstrated this.

The Big Question

If your defectiveness just keeps getting triggered, and the emotional pain keeps showing up no matter what you do, maybe trying to banish defectiveness pain isn't working. Worse, if all your attempts to cope and push away the pain create new, even more painful problems in your life, something clearly needs to change. Avoiding and coping aren't working for you. This leads to the big question: Is there another way to respond to defectiveness pain than what you've been doing? What could you do differently other than DCBs? With some creativity, could you find another path?

Creative Hopelessness

The concept of *creative hopelessness* comes out of acceptance and commitment therapy (on which this treatment program is based). The *hopelessness* part of creative hopelessness is what you've just read—the feeling that arises when you realize that all your efforts to escape defectiveness pain haven't worked; instead, they've resulted in depression and a lot of related problems. The *creative* part of creative hopelessness is the courage and new ways of thinking and acting necessary to find a different response to defectiveness pain.

If running away and avoiding the pain haven't worked, could you have a different relationship to the pain? To explore this possibility, let's consider what it's like to be stuck in quicksand. You know how quicksand works—the more you struggle, the more you sink. Thrashing and flailing—analogous to your defectiveness coping and avoidance behaviors—just pulls you deeper and deeper into the quicksand (your defectiveness pain and all your DCB-generated problems). To survive quicksand, you have to relate to it differently. Instead of trying to climb out of it, you have to get *into it*—falling forward or back—and "swimming" in the sand. What if you stopped fighting your defectiveness pain and instead learned to swim and ride the waves when it shows up?

Let's consider another metaphor. Imagine that you've fallen into a hole in the ground, surrounded by dirt (your defectiveness pain), and all you have is a shovel (your DCBs). The problem is that the more you dig with your DCBs, the deeper you get, and the more trapped you feel. You need a different relationship to the hole and the dirt in it. Instead of trying to get dirt out of the hole, *you need more dirt in it.* When you've pulled enough dirt (defectiveness pain) into the hole, it won't be a hole anymore, and you can simply walk out. We fall into defectiveness holes all the time—whenever we're triggered—and the solution is to get a little dirty (letting the pain in) so we don't get stuck.

In summary, you've got to get *in* the quicksand, *in* the dirt (defectiveness pain) so you can stop being trapped by it, and so your life can be about something other than flailing or digging. What if, instead of trying to get away from your defectiveness pain and emotions, you turned toward it, you observed it, you allowed it to be what it is? What if you stopped fighting and instead let the defectiveness pain come and go? What if you rode out these waves of pain by watching and accepting the experience whenever it came?

How Accepting Rather Than Avoiding Emotions Can Help You

To some extent, you have been a slave to your defectiveness emotions. This is a difficult truth. Every time they showed up, your reflex was always to avoid them with DCBs. It was hard to do anything else because the emotions were so painful, and your immediate habitual response was to do anything you could to try to stop the pain. You were stuck in an endless cycle: pain, avoidance, pain, avoidance.

This is called "rule-governed behavior." The rule is: when defectiveness emotions arise, you must fight and avoid them. The problem with rule-governed behavior is that it's inflexible. You just keep making the same, ineffective response over and over—even if the response (your DCBs) doesn't work, even if it makes things worse.

But, at the end of the day, the defectiveness emotions that arise *are* just emotions. Let's consider another metaphor. You could think of your emotional life as you would the sky and the weather. The sky is you—your core, unchanging self. What does change—constantly—is your emotional weather. Sometimes it's blue and clear. Sometimes there are the beautiful red-tinged clouds of a peaceful sunset. At other times, there might be angry storm clouds dumping sleet or snow—all your defectiveness-driven emotions. Or there might be fluffy banks of cumulus or a dense fog. Just like real weather, you can't choose or avoid your emotional weather. And in the same way the weather keeps changing, so also do your emotions. But what remains true through it all is that the sky (you) holds the weather (emotions), whatever they happen to be.

When defectiveness emotions (shame, sadness, fear) show up, you can watch them, accept that they are there, and let the storm slowly pass. Soon your sky will have different weather—and that, too, will pass.

Learning to watch and accept your emotional weather makes room for more flexible behavior. Instead of reflexive avoidance, you could choose entirely different responses to defectiveness emotions. You could choose, for example, just to watch the emotional weather slowly pass. Or you could respond by acting on your values, the things that really matter to you (see chapter 6), instead of being angry or withdrawn. You might choose to express your needs and feelings in the situation, seek support, learn more about the needs of the person who's triggering you, set a limit, negotiate a mutually agreeable solution, and a host of other possible responses.

Flexibility is freedom: freedom from old, habitual, and ineffective responses; freedom to do what feels right; freedom to feel what you feel; freedom to be who you *want* to be.

Responding in New Ways

Every time feelings of defectiveness show up, there is a *moment of choice* that offers real options: the old road to DCBs or a path to creative, new responses to defectiveness triggers. Once you're able to allow and accept defectiveness pain without trying to avoid it with DCBs, you are liberated to respond in new ways.

We know you're not there yet, but let's catch a glimpse of what the new ways might look like. Subsequent chapters on cultivating mindfulness (chapter 5), figuring out your values (chapter 6), learning ways to look at your thoughts like you would the weather (chapter 7), exposing yourself to the emotions you've been avoiding (chapter 9), and cultivating compassion for yourself (chapter 10) will give you tools and methods to craft these new responses. For now, let's brainstorm what some of them might be.

Right now, go back to your DCB Consequence Worksheet in chapter 3, where you recorded defectiveness triggering situations that occur in various domains of your life. List the triggers where your DCBs have the most negative consequences in the following exercise, the New Responses Worksheet. (This worksheet is also available for download at http://www .newharbinger.com/45540.) In column 2 of the worksheet, write a one-word description of your DCB for that trigger. Now, in column 3, write a possible new response. What could you do differently if your energy wasn't devoted to avoiding defectiveness pain? Who would you *want* to be in this situation? How would someone you admire act? Is there something you could do that would be more effective or more aligned with the values you hold dear? How would you treat the triggering person if you weren't caught up in pain avoidance?

New Responses Worksheet

Triggering Situation	DCB	New Alternative Responses

• *Acceptance in Action: Examples of Diane and Will*

Diane was a charter school instructor, teaching writing to unruly sixth graders. She was triggered daily by students who ignored her, talked out in class, gazed at their cell phones, or otherwise "disrespected" her. Diane was frequently angry, giving hot tongue-lashings and punishment assignments. None of her students liked her, and this only deepened her defectiveness feelings. One day she walked into her classroom, and there was a crude drawing of a witch on the blackboard. Diane exploded.

After reading a draft of the material that became this chapter, Diane realized that the defectiveness schema had been with her since she was a pudgy little girl who had trouble making friends. It never changed, and her classic response of anger never changed, either. The kids in grammar school used to tease Diane mercilessly once they knew they could get an angry rise out of her, and her sixth graders were no different now. Her defectiveness pain wasn't going to get better by trying to avoid it.

Diane considered what it would be like to allow the wave of defectiveness pain (when the kids disrespected her) and respond with something other than anger. Here is a part of Diane's New Responses Worksheet:

Triggering Situation	DCB	New Alternative Responses
Kids whispering and laughing.	Anger and attack.	Walk between them, touch their shoulders, and say, "You can talk after class."
Kid texting in class.	Anger and attack.	Just take cell phone; cheerfully say, "I'll give it back after class."
My mother complaining I haven't called.	Silence and withdrawal.	"I love you, too, Mom. So let's talk now and have a nice visit." (She'd think I'd had a stroke to say something nice.)
Kids screwing around, not doing writing assignment.	Anger and attack.	Put my hand on their shoulders and ask, "Can I help you get started?" in a kind voice.
Kid isn't doing homework.	Anger and punishment.	Ask what's getting in the way; problem solve; maybe get the parents to help.
My friend is late.	Withdrawal.	Smile, normal conversation. Bring a book next time.

Will was a painting contractor. The house painters who worked for him often failed to live up to his standards, and by now he'd just given up, letting them do a "crap job." It triggered his defectiveness pain, because the poor work seemed to reflect on him. Other triggers for Will included the state of his business (declining revenue), complaining customers, his daughter (who seemed to have no interest in him), and his girlfriend (who seemed dissatisfied and hinted at "moving on"). While Will had "surrendered" with his painters and business prospects, his reaction to his customers, daughter, and girlfriend was "seething shutdown." He was obviously angry, but he wouldn't express any of what he felt. His face would be composed into harsh angles, but his responses were usually compressed into one word. These days, everybody seemed to give him a wide berth, and Will felt increasingly alone and depressed.

After reading about avoidance and acceptance, Will realized he wasn't going to ever banish his defectiveness feelings. They would keep showing up, just as always. The same triggers would throw him into the same, familiar pain. But what if he allowed the pain and rode the emotional wave without DCBs? What if he stopped surrendering and withdrawing and chose to respond differently? Would his life and his relationships take another shape? Here is a part of Will's New Responses Worksheet.

Triggering Situation	DCB	New Alternative Response
Customer complains about paint spatters on baseboards.	Do nothing.	Apologize and send painters out to fix the problem.
Daughter doesn't greet me when I come home.	Walk in front of her, fuming.	Sit down and ask about her day; try to make contact; be interested.
Girlfriend seems distant, preoccupied with her tablet.	Look at her pointedly; walk away.	Think of something to do together; suggest it to her.
Painters leave cans and tarps behind after job is done.	Do nothing; suggest customer should throw it away.	Have painter pick the stuff up on his own time, or get it myself and deduct my time from his pay.
Girlfriend wants to take a trip by herself.	Say nothing.	Tell her how that feels to me.
Complaint: Very uneven cut-outs on molding.	Do nothing.	Inspect the problem myself, have it fixed.
Daughter talks back to me.	Walk away with open disgust.	Tell her how that feels; set limits and consequences.
Daughter stays out too late; shrugs when I ask why.	Walk away.	Consequences without anger.
"Crap job" painter gets another complaint.	Hand him the customer's message; say nothing.	Set limit; consequences such as laying him off for a week.

Chapter 5

Mindfulness

The old defectiveness-driven feelings and thoughts have made your life hard. And you've naturally tried to avoid them with defectiveness coping behaviors. In the last chapter, you explored the possibility that feelings of defectiveness don't necessarily require you to use DCBs. Instead, they can signal a choice: try to avoid the pain or accept it and respond differently.

But here's the difficulty: you have to recognize that a choice is present in order to make it. If you go on automatic pilot each time feelings of unworthiness are triggered, you'll just keep responding with your traditional DCBs. No change is possible. In order to break out of the avoidance trap, you must be able to *see the choice at the moment it occurs.* How you illuminate a moment of choice so you consciously choose one path over another requires mindfulness—the skill you'll learn in this chapter.

Mindfulness is nothing more or less than the ability to watch what's happening *now*. It's being aware of your emotions, sensations, thoughts, and urges—whether painful or pleasurable—as they occur. Mindfulness will help you notice defectiveness feelings without acting on them. It will help you recognize the urge to use DCBs. Mindfulness of the moment of choice can be learned, and we're going to start right now.

Exercise: The Five Senses

Because mindfulness begins with awareness of your experience in the present moment, one of the best ways to develop this skill is to pay attention to each of your five senses—what you see, smell, hear, taste, and feel—in sequence. This exercise will last approximately two and a half minutes, and you're encouraged to observe as many experiences as possible as you focus on each of your senses. You can record the directions below and play them back, or just read and follow each step.

Sight: Thirty Seconds

Look around and take in everything you see—the colors and shapes. . . . Notice the objects nearby . . . and then things farther away. . . . Notice bigger objects . . . and now smaller ones. . . . Just keep scanning and noticing whatever you see. . . . If your mind drifts or other thoughts arise, gently bring your attention back to everything you see.

Smell: Thirty Seconds

Now begin to notice what you can smell. Notice any fragrance or odor. . . . Can you detect wisps of soap, aftershave, or shampoo? . . . Inhale deeply to see if you can catch the faintest smell. . . . If your mind drifts or other thoughts arise, gently bring your attention back to what your nose is telling you.

Hearing: Thirty Seconds

Now pay attention to everything you can hear. Notice any voices, either nearby or at a distance . . . notice any sounds of movement . . . observe ambient sounds—like the hum of a refrigerator or an air conditioner. . . . Your own body may make sounds—perhaps breathing or swallowing—and you can notice those as well. . . . Observe any distant sounds—of birds or passing cars. . . . If your mind drifts or other thoughts arise, gently bring your attention back to what you are hearing.

Taste: Thirty Seconds

Now bring your attention to whatever you can taste. There may be traces of things you recently drank or ate. . . . There may be the faintest sense of sweet or sour. . . . Lick your finger and notice the slight salty taste. . . . If your mind drifts to other things or other thoughts intrude, gently bring your attention back to your sense of taste.

Touch: Thirty Seconds

Now turn your attention to sensations of touch. Notice feelings of pressure or heaviness where your body touches the floor or the chair. . . . Notice the temperature of the air. . . . Observe what your hands are touching—is it smooth or rough? . . . Notice where you're touched by the clothes you wear. . . . If your mind drifts or other thoughts show up, gently return your attention to your sense of touch.

During the "five senses" exercise, as with all mindfulness processes, thoughts will periodically intrude and distract you from observing your sensations. This is normal. Sometimes the thoughts will come at you rapid-fire, and at other times, thoughts will surface more slowly. The object is to notice thoughts as soon as you can and shift attention back to what you see, smell, hear, taste, or feel.

This introductory mindfulness experience will deepen your ability to observe the moment, bringing awareness to whatever is happening right now. Ultimately, it can help you recognize the moment of choice as you get used to noticing your experience as it unfolds. We suggest that you do the "five senses" once a day for the next week as part of your introduction to mindfulness.

Exercise: Mindful Focusing

This exercise strengthens your ability to observe the moment without struggling, avoiding, or resisting.* You'll learn to watch thoughts, sensations, and emotions as they arise and see them for what they are—transient experiences that come and go in your awareness and that require no response on your part. You can watch them without having to do anything. You can choose to record and play back the directions below or simply read and meditate on the following.

Close your eyes and take a deep breath . . . and notice the experience of breathing. Observe perhaps the feeling of coolness as the breath passes through your nose or down the back of your throat. . . . Notice the sensation of your ribs expanding, the air entering your lungs. . . . Be aware of your diaphragm stretching with the breath . . . and of the feeling of release as you exhale.

Just keep watching your breath, letting your attention move along the path of flowing air . . . in and out . . . in and out. As you breathe, you will also notice other experiences. You may be aware of thoughts; when a thought comes up, just say to yourself, *thought*. Just label it for what it is: thought. And if you're aware of a sensation, whatever it is, just say to yourself, *sensation*. And if you notice an emotion, just say to yourself, *emotion*. Just label it for what it is: emotion.

Try not to hold on to any experience. Just label it and let it go. And wait for the next experience. You are just watching your mind and body while labeling thoughts, sensations, and emotions. If something feels painful, just note the pain and remain open to the next thing that comes up. Keep watching each experience, whatever it is, labeling it and letting it pass in order to be open for what comes next.

Let it all happen as you watch: thoughts . . . sensations . . . feelings. It's all just weather, while you are the sky. Just passing weather . . . something to watch . . . and label . . . and let go. (Continue the meditation for two additional minutes.)

---

*   The exercise is adapted from Matthew McKay, Patrick Fanning, Avigail Lev, and Michelle L. Skeen, *The Interpersonal Problems Workbook: ACT to End Painful Relationship Patterns* (Oakland, CA: New Harbinger Publications, 2013).

After doing mindful focusing for a week or two, you may notice changes in how you relate to inner experiences. Labeling experiences *thought, sensation,* or *emotion* can create some distance, perhaps even a degree of separation between you and what you experience. Mindful focusing can also increase your willingness to let even painful experiences run their course without judging or trying to stop what happens.

Mindful Activities

Mindfulness can be much more than watching your inner experience. It can be practiced by closely observing ordinary activities like eating or walking or even teeth brushing. Instead of doing them in the usual way—distracted and unattended—you can learn to perform these tasks with full awareness. It's completely normal, during mindfulness activities, for random thoughts to intrude. Just note the thought and as soon as possible return attention to your sensory experience. Below are some examples of mindful activities.

Mindful Walking. Set a specific time each day for mindful walking—perhaps to and from work, or an evening stroll around your neighborhood. Notice the pressure of your feet on the ground and the swing of each leg. Feel the air pressing against your face along with the sights, sounds, and smells as you move. Notice the sway of your hands and your shifting balance. Perhaps count each step.

Mindful Tooth Brushing. Notice the sensation of the bristles against your gums. Observe the flavor of the toothpaste. Feel the movement of your hand and arm, the pressure of the brush against your fingers. Feel the coolness of the water as you rinse.

Mindful Showering. Notice the sound of the water. Feel the warmth and sensation of the spray on various parts of your body. Notice the slippery soap and the texture of the washcloth.

A Mindful Cup of Tea or Coffee. Notice the warmth and the texture of the cup in your hand, and the sensation of the steam and heat rising. Notice the smell and the taste. Observe the feelings in your mouth, and your throat, and the warmth in your stomach.

Mindful Eating. Start with something simple, like a sandwich, and work your way up to a plate of varied foods. Notice the texture of the food, the taste, the temperature. Notice the smell. Now observe the sensation of lifting your utensil. Notice each mouthful—the sensation of chewing, moving food with your tongue, and swallowing.

Mindful Dishwashing. Notice the warm water, the slippery soap, the hard edges of the dishes, the pressure of the sponge, and the movement of your arm. Listen to the sound of the running tap. Feel your body flex as you bend to put plates in the dishwasher.

Mindful Gardening. Notice the cool feel of the soil, the thrust of pushing down the trowel. Notice the smell of flowers and earth. Feel the tug as you're pulling weeds.

Other examples are mindful driving, exercising, shopping, cooking, and so forth. Start with two mindful activities in the first week, and add two more in each succeeding week until you have at least six daily activities that you focus on mindfully. The goal is to stay more and more with your sensory experience and strengthen the skill of self-observation.

• *Starr's Mindful Practice*

Starr struggled with sadness and self-critical thoughts after a breakup three years ago. Her mindfulness practice seemed hard to do at first because the sadness showed up almost immediately. Each time she noticed feelings of depression she'd say to herself, there's an emotion. *Sometimes there were threads of anger woven into the sadness. Again, she'd say,* there's another emotion.

Alongside the emotion were related thoughts—mostly negative judgments about herself. There's a thought, *she'd say to herself. Sometimes the thoughts slowed down, and sometimes they quickly followed one after another.* Thought . . . thought . . . thought— *she just kept labeling them.*

The sadness often seemed connected to a heavy feeling in Starr's stomach, and she would label that, too, when it occurred: feeling. *As she became more skilled at watching and naming her experience, Starr felt less involved in her thoughts and emotions. She described it simply:* Okay, fine, I'm having this emotion, this thought. Let's see what happens next. *She began to feel—during practice sessions—a sense of detachment from inner experience.* I'm having this feeling, then this thought, then the next and the next. It doesn't seem so important; I can just watch one moment roll into the next.

As her ability to watch internal experiences strengthened, Starr launched into several mindful activities, including mindful walking and mindful exercising. Twice each day she walked seven blocks between the subway and work. She counted her steps up to ten and then started over. She observed the sensations of movement in her arms and legs, and she noticed the feel of the air and the pressure of her feet against the pavement. Also, each day, Starr observed her stair machine exercise at the gym. While she additionally did stretches and weight lifting, she used mindfulness awareness—at first—with a single type of exercise.

Over the weeks, Starr added mindful eating and drinking, as well as showering and things like making a salad. As her mindfulness became more practiced and second nature, Starr noticed several changes. She was more able to observe when thoughts—especially ones of shame or defectiveness—intruded, and it was easier for her to refocus on the activity at hand. Furthermore, she began to feel calmer and more aware of what was happening in the moment. She said the difference was profound: "I feel awake, very aware of what I'm feeling and doing. It's a serious change."

Recognizing Defectiveness Triggers

Now it's time to use mindful awareness to recognize the moment your defectiveness feelings get triggered. Because if you can see that old emotional pain when it shows up, you can also see the moment of choice—to fall back into those depression-making DCBs or not.

To practice this important skill, go back to the DCB Consequence Worksheet in chapter 3. If you haven't yet filled it out, list as many defectiveness-triggering situations as you can in the left-hand column. Note that triggering events can include thoughts and memories, as well as things that happen between you and others. Then, on the worksheet below, describe the feelings, thoughts, and urges that most commonly arise across these many triggers. (This worksheet is also available for download at http://www.newharbinger.com/45540.)

Defectiveness Response Profile

Most Common Feelings:

Most Common Thoughts:

Most Common Urges—DCBs:

Do you remember Will, the painting contractor from chapter 4? When he reviewed his list of triggering situations, his defectiveness emotions, thoughts, and urges could be distilled into the following summary.

Will's Defectiveness Response Profile

Most Common Feelings:

Worthless, ashamed, failure, not valued, unloved, disrespected.

Most Common Thoughts:

I've screwed everything up. No one cares about me. All is lost. Everything I touch goes wrong. I should just give up.

Most Common Urges—DCBs:

Ignore whatever it is and do nothing. Say nothing. Walk away. Withdraw.

Building Mindfulness for the Moment of Choice: The Morning Intention

Once you've completed your profile, the next steps are to (1) remember it, and (2) commit to recognizing when these feelings, thoughts, and urges arise in daily life. You can achieve this through a technique called the Morning Intention. Here's what you do: each morning at a set time (such as over coffee or right after getting dressed), review your profile of defectiveness-driven feelings, thoughts, and urges. Read every word and briefly try to hold what this experience is like for you. Then commit to yourself, with a strong intention, that you will do two things for the rest of the day:

- Watch for any emergence of these feelings, thoughts, and urges during the day.

- Should they get triggered, remember that this is your moment of choice. You can choose to respond with old action urges (DCBs). Or you can do something else—including one of the alternative responses you developed in chapter 4.

Even if you sometimes fall back to coping with your old strategies, the important thing is noticing that moment in time when you could possibly take a different path. Right now, success is awareness, not necessarily stopping the old DCB. Throughout this book, including the next chapter, which is on values, you'll learn more and more alternatives to DCBs. So right now, just notice the moment where there's a fork in the road. Which road you take—at the moment—isn't crucially important.

• *Will's Morning Intention*

Will was reluctant to do the morning intention practice. It was triggering to read his profile. The words themselves seemed to elicit defectiveness feelings. Yet at the same time, he knew something had to change. His DCBs were only making him more depressed. With some hesitation on the first morning, he read over the profile documented above. The words evoked sadness and feelings of failure. But he read them anyway and committed to observing any defectiveness triggers throughout the day.

On day one, he completely lost track. He got triggered by his daughter and one of his employees and didn't even notice. He made the same commitment on day two, and that day he did notice it, but only after slumping away when his daughter said something hurtful. On day three, he noticed the trigger when it happened, but did his DCB anyway. However, Will recognized this as progress.

On day four, one of his painters left spatters on a customer's rug. He almost told the woman to just fix it and send him the bill. He felt himself collapsing. Yet he now was aware that a choice could be made: give up or insist his painters do things the right way. He decided to send his employee back to clean up the site. That evening, his daughter refused to get off her phone to do homework—she said he was bothering her. In response, Will poured himself a bourbon, neat. He still had a way to go, but on day five, Will still made a commitment to his morning intentions.

Watching What Happens

When your defectiveness pain is triggered, try to do one thing: watch without acting on DCBs. Observe what's happening emotionally while trying not to react habitually.

- Notice the feelings.

- Notice the thoughts.

- Notice sensations.

- Notice your impulses.

- Notice that you have a choice.

An important tool for strengthening your power to choose is keeping a diary of triggering events. The diary can, after the fact, deepen your awareness of each part of the experience. And, during later triggering events, your diary can sharpen your ability to observe—without using DCBs—your hard-to-feel emotions. (This diary is also available for download at http://www.newharbinger.com/45540.)

Triggering Events Diary

Event: _____

- Emotions: _____
- Thoughts: _____
- Physical sensations: _____
- Urges: _____
- Check one: ☐ Acted on urge   ☐ Didn't act on urge

Result: _____

_____

Event: _____

- Emotions: _____
- Thoughts: _____
- Physical sensations: _____
- Urges: _____
- Check one: ☐ Acted on urge   ☐ Didn't act on urge

Result: _____

_____

Event: _____

- Emotions: _____
- Thoughts: _____
- Physical sensations: _____
- Urges: _____
- Check one: ☐ Acted on urge   ☐ Didn't act on urge

Result: _____

_____

Event: _____

- Emotions: _____
- Thoughts: _____
- Physical sensations: _____
- Urges: _____
- Check one: ☐ Acted on urge   ☐ Didn't act on urge

Result: _____

_____

Diane's Triggering Events Diary

Event: A child in my class shrugs when I ask where his homework is.

- Emotions: Anger. I'm feeling disrespected.

- Thoughts: He doesn't care. I'm not reaching him; I'm a lousy teacher.

- Physical sensations: Tight, sick feeling in stomach.

- Urges: Yell that he's failing. Make threats.

- Check one: ☑ Acted on urge   ☐ Didn't act on urge

Result: The child just smirked at me. I felt helpless, depressed, a failure.

Event: My friend cancels lunch.

- Emotions: Hurt, sadness, feeling of being less than.

- Thoughts: She doesn't care. She doesn't like me. There's something wrong with me as a friend.

- Physical sensations: Tight, sick feeling in gut.

- Urges: Send text saying we're done as friends; blasting her for being so inconsiderate.

- Check one: ☐ Acted on urge   ☑ Didn't act on urge

Result: Waited a day. Texted I missed her and asked her to suggest other dates for lunch. (Kind of a test.) She set a new date. Felt less hurt, sad.

Event: Boyfriend's apartment was a mess when I came over.

- Emotions: Feel insulted that he doesn't value me enough to clean up. Hurt. Angry. Depressed.

- Thoughts: He doesn't care. I'm stupid to be in this relationship.

- Physical sensations: Feel hot, tight.

- Urges: Blast him for keeping his place a mess; threaten to go home.

- Check one: ☐ Acted on urge ☑ Didn't act on urge

Result: Told him it upset and hurt me that he invited me into a mess. He apologized. I felt less depressed.

Event: A kid in class says "time to go" and walks out.

- Emotions: Shame—he has no respect. Anger.

- Thoughts: This kid is f****d up. How dare he. This is wrong.

- Physical sensations: Hot.

- Urges: Run after him down the hall screaming and threatening suspension.

- Check one: ☑ Acted on urge ☐ Didn't act on urge

Result: Kid ran away. Principal counseled me for behaving unprofessionally. Very depressed.

Event: Remembering the principal's reprimand.

- Emotions: Shame, depression.

- Thoughts: I'm a failure.

- Physical sensations: Stomach tight, sick feeling. Also tight in chest.

- Urges: Threaten to quit. Demand that I get more support with difficult class. Criticize the principal.

- Check one: ☐ Acted on urge ☑ Didn't act on urge

Result: Wrote hand-written apology for my behavior. Expressed overwhelm with difficult class; asked for problem-solving conference. Felt apprehensive, but a little hopeful.

Diane's diary, as you can see, had mixed results. But she learned something from every event—in particular, that her depression got worse when she acted on her DCB urges. And there was something else: she understood that sometimes it was possible to choose a different path from old, habitual ways of coping.

Chapter 6

Values

Values are an important point in your journey to overcome depression. You've learned, in the last chapter on mindfulness, how to begin observing the painful triggering situations that set off feelings of defectiveness and shame and the action urge that goes with them. Noticing the action urge is crucial, because that urge to withdraw, to get angry, to avoid, or to give up in the face of a defectiveness trigger—as understandable as it is with all that shame—has made you pull back from life. It's what's keeping you depressed. Seeing the urge to erase defectiveness shame, at the moment it occurs, changes everything. Because if you can see the urge to start those old defectiveness coping behaviors, you can also see the moment of choice. You can recognize the exact moment when you might do something else.

Trouble is, right now your only choice is to do—or not do—those depression-feeding coping behaviors. This chapter is about giving you new, positive choices to make when shame strikes, when those old defectiveness feelings make you want to withdraw, get angry, give up, or numb out. This new option is to act on your values—the things you care about and who and how you want to be on this planet.

Of course, in order to act on your values, you have to know what those are. That's what we'll do in this chapter.

What Are Values?

Values are the direction you want to take in life; they are a compass that points to what matters. Your values are also a guiding light for who you want to be and how you want to act in the meaningful domains of living, like your work, leisure time, and relationships. They prescribe ideal behavior, encouraging a person to be, for example, caring, honest, supportive, protective, productive, creative, committed to learning, loyal, or honorable.

Notice that values can often be described in one or two words. The reason is because they offer directions, not detailed instructions for getting there. They offer the priority, say, of being understanding and supportive of your daughter—but don't tell you exactly what to do when she puts crayon marks on the wall. And they're not goals. You can never reach or achieve a value. You don't arrive at a moment in life where you have achieved openness and honesty; rather, these are qualities that a person might strive for in relationships. Again, values are a heading, some true north of what person we want to be—not a place we reach saying, "Done! Cross that off the list."

However, it's true that in order to act on your values, you need to set goals that are in line with them—or rather, intentions. *Intentions* are how we enact values in specific situations. They're ways we turn values into action at a specific time and place. The following chart shows the distinction between values and goals.

Notice how the values are things to strive for that can never be reached. The goals, on the other hand—which reflect this person's values—are all achievable in a particular time frame.

When you engage in DCBs, they take you away from your values and intentions. Your life is about avoiding defectiveness pain instead of doing what you care about. That's why clarifying your values and acting on them can begin to liberate you from the trap of defectiveness avoidance and all the depression it creates. Now that we know what values are, let's figure out yours.

Values and Goals

Value	Goal
Keep family safe	• Buy a house.
	• Get security system.
	• Save $500 per month.
Be supportive	• Help brother fix his car.
	• Ask friend about his problem at work.
	• Help daughter with civics assignment.
Learning	• Read Yuval Noah Harari's *Sapiens*.
	• Take parenting class.
	• Get a consult on our garden.
Productive	• Finish new website for work.
	• Clean side yard.
	• Find gymnastics program for daughter.
Be healthy	• Exercise four times a week for one half hour.
	• Set up no-carb diet.
	• Set up doctor appointment for physical.
Peacefulness	• Go to Slater Falls this weekend.
	• Get music headphones.
	• Do ten minutes of mindfulness each morning.

Clarifying Your Values

As a starting point for mapping your most important values, fill in the worksheet below. The worksheet is composed of a list of ten life domains: intimate relationships, parenting, education and learning, friends and social life, self-care and physical health, family of origin (meaning parents, siblings, and so forth), spirituality, community life and citizenship, leisure and recreation, work and career, and "other." Under the header "Important," put a check mark to identify any domains that represent significant parts of your life. Next, under each *important* domain, write one or two words to describe the value that matters most for you in this area of life. This value represents who you want to be and how you want to behave in that domain. Finally, under the header "Intention," identify one specific situation in which you could turn the value into action. This action, motivated by your value, would be a way to express it in a particular time or place, or with a specific individual.

Think carefully about your intentions. For each domain, select intentions to do things you've been avoiding because of your fear of feeling defective or ashamed. For example, let's say you have a value of *understanding your partner*, who seems stressed and sad lately. But shame has kept you from asking because you're afraid of being told it's your fault. A good intention for this domain would be choosing a time when you are both relaxed, and you could ask how your partner is feeling. (This worksheet is also available for download at http://www.newharbinger.com/45540.)

Values Clarification Worksheet

Important	Domain and Value	Intention (goal)
	Intimate relationships V:	
	Parenting V:	
	Education and learning V:	
	Friends and social life V:	
	Self-care and physical health V:	
	Family of origin V:	
	Spirituality V:	

Important	Domain and Value	Intention (goal)
	Community life and citizenship V:	
	Leisure and recreation V:	
	Work and career V:	
	Other: V:	
	Other: V:	
	Other: V:	

Review what you've written on the Values Clarification Worksheet. How many of your important values are you acting on? Rate each value from 1 to 5 (where 1 means you *never* act on that value, and 5 means you act on it *nearly every day*). Note and circle your rating next to each value.

Now review your intentions. Each intention should offer a means to enact your values in a particular domain, and include all of the following:

- An opportunity to do something that your fear of shame and your DCBs have blocked or made difficult to do.

- An opportunity to respond differently from your old DCBs.

- An opportunity to behave in ways that are aligned with who you want to be and can support your sense of worth.

- A stretch, but doable—something challenging, and yet doesn't trigger an overwhelming level of fear.

As you review your intentions, rewrite or revise any that don't meet the above criteria. And try to decide exactly when, where, and with whom you'll carry out every intention.

Each week make a new list of intentions on the Values Clarification Weekly Update Worksheet (a copy is just below, and you can find it in downloadable form at http://www.newharbinger.com/45540). Keep the intentions that require more time to act on or that need additional efforts to complete. Replace ones you've completed—or if you conclude you're not ready to try them—with new goals. Make notes about what you did or didn't do. As before, make these intentions explicit, planning when, where, and with whom you'll carry them out. The more care you take in planning your intentions, the more likely they'll actually happen.

Over the weeks, you may decide to focus on different values for a particular intention. You may include intentions that aren't specifically blocked by fears of shame and defectiveness, but that you've had difficulty acting on for other reasons. But this much is important: during the whole process of your recovery from depression, your focus—week after week—needs to be about turning your values into action.

Values Clarification Weekly Update Worksheet

Week: _____ Update

Domain and Value	Intention and Notes

Values-Based Intentions and Recovery

You became depressed because your life evolved into being about avoiding shame and defectiveness feelings. You became less and less the person you wanted to be as you engaged in more avoidance and more DCBs. There is the basic choice in life: doing what matters, doing what you care about, or having your days focused on trying to escape pain.

You already know that trying to avoid shame and defectiveness doesn't work. But what it does do is rob your life of valued activities and pave a royal road to depression. It's a totally understandable trap; humans are conditioned to avoid pain. But in trying to escape shame and defectiveness, your life has lost its purpose. So many of the things you care about and value have been diminished. This is how we get depressed. And this is why a daily commitment to values-based intentions is so important.

If losing sight of what matters generates depression, acting—every day—on your values-based intentions is how you recover. There may still be *moments* of shame, and those old defectiveness feelings may *temporarily* loom up—but you will no longer endure the dead weight of depression. You'll feel fully alive and vital again for one reason: your days are about what you value and not what you avoid.

• *Rebekah*

Consider Rebekah, who has been struggling with serious depression since shortly after graduating from college six years ago. She works nights serving drinks at a comedy club but is often so depressed that she has to force herself to get there. She sleeps until the afternoon, eats fast food, and surfs the internet until the club opens. Once or twice a week, Rebekah has sex with Barry, a "friend with benefits" who is the publicist at the club. She'd like to have more of a relationship but fears asking because, she says, "I think Barry wants something better." She's thought of internet dating, but the embarrassment of "looking like you need that" triggers her shame.

Rebekah has dreams of taking comedy-writing classes, developing her own comedy sketches, and trying them out on open mic nights at the club. But each of those ideas generates fear. She did, about a year ago, do a brief stint on open mic night. Her material got some laughs, but in Rebekah's mind not enough. She burned with shame afterward.

With friends, Rebekah feels she "has to put on a good show." However, her depression makes it harder to pull this off. "They'll get what a mess I am." She fears friends will see through her joking, lighthearted style to the "bullshit underneath." All this leads her more and more to withdraw from friends, or "be as phony as a three-dollar bill." In college Rebekah often went mountain biking with friends, but she is reluctant to ride or join a cycling club now because of embarrassment about her stamina.

Rebekah grew up with a brother, Eli, who is on the autism spectrum, and at times she has wanted to volunteer or even work with autistic kids. But she is afraid of doing things wrong or using techniques she learned with her brother that professionals might laugh at. Her fear of shame even makes her hesitant to call her brother "because it's so hard to think of things to say."

When Rebekah graduated from college, she had a lot of hope. But life evolved to be about avoidance of her defectiveness feelings. The things that mattered—close friendships, a committed relationship, making people laugh, creativity, physical health, a caring relationship with her brother, and helping kids with autism—were gradually lost and her depression deepened. She began to see herself as someone who had failed, and her judgmental thoughts rose to a cacophony.

Below you'll find Rebekah's first Values Clarification Worksheet. And then you'll see her revised intentions for several weeks following. Being consistent with your values work is crucial to recovery. Doing the initial worksheet isn't enough. Keep working on the weekly updates, adding new intentions as you go, until values-based activities are peppered throughout your week. And, most important, until your depression has lifted significantly.

Rebekah's Values Clarification Worksheet

Important	Domain and Value	Intention (goal)
2	Intimate relationships V: Be supportive and kind	• Put up dating profile. • Help Barry find a doctor for dizzy spells.
	Parenting V:	
1	Education and learning V: Learn about comedy, treating autism	• Register for class on comedy writing. • Investigate behavior analyst graduate programs.
2	Friends and social life V: Be close, connected	• Tell Julie about my struggle with depression; initiate a lunch date.
1	Self-care and physical health V: Be strong; have stamina	• One-hour bike ride Tuesday. • Investigate co-ed cycling clubs.
1	Family of origin V: Be supportive and caring	• Call Eli, see how he is—Wednesday night (hard to talk to him).
	Spirituality V:	
	Community life and citizenship V:	
2	Leisure and recreation V: Laughter	• Watch stand-up comedy (Netflix)
1	Work and career V: Help people laugh	• Do open mic night next week.
2	Other: V: Creativity	• Finish one seven-minute sketch. (Work on it Monday and Thursday evenings.)

Rebekah's Values Clarification Worksheet

Week _2_ Update

Domain and Value	Intention and Notes
Intimate relationships	• Respond to two messages from guys on dating website. • Find doctor for Barry (even though we broke up).
Education and learning	• Didn't register for comedy class—missed cutoff date. • Study online brochures for behavior analyst M.A. program at Northwestern.
Friends and social life	• Told Julie about my depression. • Made date to hike Sunday afternoon with Julie, Joan, and Laura. • Cookout at Julie's Thursday—they're doing it on my night off.
Self-care and physical health	• Did bike ride alone. • Cycling club does Saturday bike rides—didn't sign up.
Family of origin	• Called Eli—felt good. • Call Dad on his b-day.
Leisure and recreation	• Watched comedy. It's hard, 'cause they're so good, so far above me. • Watch again—learn something.
Work and career	• Didn't do open mic. • Rehearse my new material with Julie.
Creativity	• Keep working on seven-minute sketch (Monday and Thursday evenings).

Rebekah's Values Clarification Worksheet

Week _3_ Update

Domain and Value	Intention and Notes
Intimate relationships	• Didn't like the guys' messages. • Respond to two more messages on dating website. • Found doctor for Barry; agreed we care about each other as friends. • Ask for the truth about how he really sees me (totally terrified).
Education and learning	• Call Northwestern to talk to an advisor.
Friends and social life	• Make date to bike ride with Julie. Tell about my recovery plan. • Get comps for my friends to comedy club; go out after we close.
Self-care and physical health	• Sign up for Saturday bike ride.
Family of origin	• Called Dad. He suggested a visit—not ready. • Promised to call Mom this week.
Leisure and recreation	• Watched another stand-up performance. Made notes on timing. • Watch all of John Mulaney. Figure out what makes him funny. Imitate.
Work and career	• Did open mic (just five minutes). One joke really killed them. Very anxious, but okay after.
Creativity	• Finished my sketch—used part of it for open mic. Put together five more minutes of material using John Mulaney topics.

Planning for the Moment of Choice

So far you've been working on having your life aligned with values rather than pain avoidance. Now it's time to get back to those defectiveness-triggering situations that keep pushing you to withdraw, get angry, give up, or numb out—all the behaviors that deepen depression. This is an opportunity to plan values-based intentions for each shame-triggering situation. On the Triggers and Intentions Worksheet (see below), list all the shame and defectiveness triggers you've experienced in the past month. In the second column, Defectiveness Coping Behaviors, write what you did to try to avoid the shame and feelings of defectiveness. In the third column, write the relevant value for this situation. And finally, in the last column, write a specific intention for how you could act on your value when this triggering situation arises again. (This worksheet is also available for download at http://www.newharbinger.com/45540.)

Below the blank Triggers and Intentions Worksheet, you'll find one that Rebekah filled out. We encourage you to look at her example, so you have a better feel for completing your own.

Triggers and Intentions Worksheet

Shame and Defectiveness Triggers	Defectiveness Coping Behaviors	Values	Specific Intentions

Rebekah's Triggers and Intentions Worksheet

Shame and Defectiveness Triggers	Defectiveness Coping Behaviors	Values	Specific Intentions
Barry criticizes my makeup.	Angrily wash it all off; pout.	Kindness Assertiveness	Tell him nicely that I like how I look.
People complain about the drink.	Get huffy; ignore them.	Responsive to others' needs. Kindness.	Kindly ask about the problem. Understand it; fix it.
Feel embarrassed about how slow I am, falling behind with the cycling club.	Give up; go back home.	Persistence. Strength. Relationships.	Ask in advance if someone would stay with me if I fall behind.
Embarrassed when Northwestern advisor asked questions I didn't know how to answer about behavior analysis.	Quickly got off the phone. Didn't learn much.	Learn something useful. Honesty.	Call back with questions. Admit I don't know much about behavior analysis.
Dead spaces (no laughter) during open mic stand-up.	Stopped early. Told friends I was bad (but I wasn't, really).	Persistence. Give people laughter.	Do it in two weeks— the whole seven minutes.
Practicing my stand-up routine with Julie— she doesn't like one of the jokes.	Got angry, defensive. Cut it short.	Honesty.	Admit I feel vulnerable. Maybe rewrite the joke. Keep practicing.
A guy messages me saying he wants to meet me.	Procrastinate writing back. Think of a bunch of reasons not to meet him.	A close relationship with someone. Kindness.	Set up a coffee date. Email him today.

As new situations occur, keep updating your Triggers and Intentions Worksheet. This process is important for your recovery from depression, because it helps you do the opposite of the old avoidance and defectiveness coping strategies. Every time you notice a shame or defectiveness avoidance behavior, think it through: What is your value in this situation? How could you act on the value next time?

Commitment and Willingness

Pivoting away from old coping behaviors, away from depression and toward your values, will require commitment. A commitment, to be real and to last, is the intention to do something (your values-based action) with full willingness to experience and face whatever barriers show up. In other words, a commitment means you are willing to have worry thoughts or self-judging thoughts, and to feel shame and fear, in whatever form or intensity, and still *act on your values.*

As you plan and act on your values-based intentions, think about your willingness. Are you willing to face whatever barriers show up, whatever shame or painful thoughts, and act on your intention anyway? Try to choose intentions where you are 100 percent willing to feel and face whatever happens.

There is no such thing as a little willingness or partial willingness. It's not true willingness to say, "I'll do X as long as my shame doesn't go above 5 on a 10-point scale." Or, in Rebekah's case, "I'm willing to perform at open mic as long as I don't get too embarrassed." Willingness is always 100 percent. It requires us to accept all of the emotion and every painful thought in the service of doing the things that matter to us.

The Values Path

The values path is a metaphor to explain willingness and how it helps you overcome depression. Imagine a mountain path that climbs steeply into a craggy, lonely landscape. The path leads to something important to you, something you value. But you will have to climb this by yourself; no one else can do it for you.

On the following page is a representation of this path. At the top, write a value and particular intention (something that challenges you). That's where you're headed. The trouble is that this path is hard. There are barriers:

- self-judging thoughts

- worry thoughts

- feelings of depression with the urge to withdraw

- doubt

- shame

- fear

- tiredness or exhaustion

You will face most or all of these on the climb. They are unavoidable, and you will find them lying across the path. Right now, write in the barriers you expect to face on the climb toward your value and chosen intention. Imagine actually carrying out your intention. Visualize yourself in the situation and notice what emotions come up. Notice your thoughts. Notice how your body feels. Keep visualizing yourself acting on the intention, and capture all that you feel and think on the values path graphic.

Now it's time to consider your choices. If the barriers feel too challenging, there's a fork at the bottom of the path. You could veer off toward avoidance and defectiveness coping behaviors (DCBs). For a moment, let's take that path and see what happens. Think about this: What occurs if you continue to avoid acting on your value? What will your life look like? Will it affect your work or your relationships? Will avoidance of this value stir painful emotions? Will avoidance affect how you see and feel about yourself? How will it impact your depression, your confidence, your health? Try to identify as many avoidance outcomes as you can and write them in the space provided on the graphic.

Avoidance has a cost. Consider how long you'll have to pay this price. A few days? Months? Years?

Valuer Path

Value: _____

Intention: _____

Barrier: _____

Barrier: _____

Barrier: _____

Barrier: _____

Barrier: _____

Barrier: _____

All right, let's go back to the fork in the road. The values path is littered with worry, self-judgment, doubt, shame, and other barriers. You can't get around them. How do you get to your values with these thoughts and feelings in the way? The only way would be to pick them up and take them with you on the climb. And to keep climbing while carrying the shame, the exhaustion, the doubt, the depression-driven urge to quit, and the defectiveness feelings. You have to carry whatever barriers show up on the path if you want to be the person who lives that value.

So that's the choice—carrying the pain with you in the direction of what matters or living with the avoidance outcomes. Willingness means you will carry whatever painful thoughts or feelings block the path so you can live your value. Overcoming depression demands willingness, and that you make the choice. These are some of the barriers you will face:

- Self-judging, self-denigrating thoughts about what's wrong with you and how everybody can see it. These are painful and sometimes paralyzing. The sense is being wrong and bad *plus* being exposed.

- Worry thoughts. These thoughts project into the future and assume your values-based actions will be met with contempt, judgment, or rejection.

- Shame, fear, and depression, including how these emotions show up in your body. In many cases, the fear of shame is more painful and inhibiting than the shame itself. And depression-triggered exhaustion is very hard, as well. These emotions have an action urge that makes us want to run. It's hardwired in us. But acting on that urge is driving your depression.

If you need help with those barriers, the next three chapters will give you tools to overcome each one. Chapter 7, "Defusion," will help you gain distance and detachment from self-judging and worry thoughts. Chapter 8, "Avoidance and Exposure," and chapter 9, "Facing Your Shame and Sadness," will strengthen you to better tolerate fear and shame when they arise. If barriers are sometimes getting in the way of your intentions, these new tools will help you do what matters.

We will help you every step of the way.

Chapter 7

Defusion

In this chapter you will learn a powerful mental technique called "defusion," which will help you deal with the worry and self-judging thoughts that might come up as you act on your values-based intentions, which typically drive you to your DCBs. The term "defusion" was coined by Steve Hayes, the developer of acceptance and commitment therapy. He noticed that unhappy people tend to be "fused" to their negative thoughts, unable to separate their core identity from their transitory train of thought. He began looking for ways that people could "un-fuse" or "de-fuse" themselves from their distressing thoughts.

When you try to act on values-based intentions in the face of shame and defectiveness, thoughts will come up. And all these thoughts will *feel* true in some way. You *think* things like *I'm stupid, I'm worthless,* and *I'm crazy*—and you feel that that means you must *be* stupid or worthless or crazy.

This chapter will explain why this is not true. It will explain how all kinds of thoughts arise, occupy the mind for a while, and pass out of consciousness. It will teach you several defusion methods for distancing yourself from your more negative thoughts, thereby distancing yourself from the emotional pain they cause. When you can consistently notice, label, and let go of defectiveness thoughts, it relieves some of the sadness they cause and frees you to concentrate on your intentions and what is really important to you in your life.

Your Mind as Survival Mechanism

The human mind has evolved primarily as a survival mechanism. It is designed to keep you safe and alive long enough to produce offspring and continue the human race. It does this by constantly monitoring all your sense impressions: what you see, hear, smell, taste, and feel. Your mind is always scanning the environment for danger, looking for the cave bear, the cliff edge, the speeding car running a stoplight, or your algebra teacher's disappointed look.

Your mind turns your sense impressions, especially sense impressions of risk or danger, into the mental language we call thoughts. Thoughts can take many forms—predictions, stories, judgments, reasons, comparisons, justifications, assumptions, opinions, theories, questions, images, ideas, doubts, evaluations, and so on. Your mind is a thought-creating machine that you cannot turn off. It is designed to scan the environment and churn out thoughts constantly, and here's the real kicker: the topics and frequency of these thoughts are not really under your control.

For example, Alana was a junior college student who wanted to be a nurse—but she worried she might not be able to keep up with the coursework. As she read about the nursing curriculum online, her mind turned what she saw on the screen into a stream of negative thoughts:

- *I'll never get in.* (prediction)

- *Rachel got in, wasted two years, and finally flunked out.* (story, comparison)

- *It's too hard to be a nurse.* (judgment)

- *I don't have what it takes.* (opinion)

- *Dental hygiene would be shorter and easier.* (theory)

- *White smock, mask, and eye shield.* (image)

- *Are teeth less icky than blood?* (evaluation, question)

- *I just don't know what to do.* (doubt)

- *I'll never memorize all that anatomy stuff.* (prediction)

- *Dad already thinks I'm a ditz.* (assumption)

- *This is too stressful.* (judgment)

- *I'll look again tomorrow when I'm fresher.* (justification)

This list looks somewhat organized and logical, laid out on the page as it is. But imagine these thoughts flashing through Alana's mind, much faster than you can read them. And many of these thoughts were repeated several times, with variations and as fragmentary phrases. Her survival-oriented mind was trying to steer her away from the risky, dangerous path of attempting something new and challenging, where the stakes would be high and the chance of failure real. For that evening at least, Alana's negative thoughts drowned out her desire to succeed in school, to do something worthwhile, to help other people, and to feel good about herself.

Your survival mind operates in three ways. Sometimes it's like a bus full of monsters: you're trying to drive the bus to where you want to go, and there are monsters in the back—your shame and fear and defectiveness—screaming at you: "No, it's too risky! It's too hard that way!" "Look out!" "Turn back! Go an easier way!" The monsters don't shut up; in fact, the more you try to placate and please the monsters, the louder and rowdier they become.

The second way your survival mind operates is like a pushy salesperson dedicated to pushing the merchandise, to getting you to buy into the same old shoddy goods of self-doubt and hopelessness—even if you no longer want them: "You'll never amount to anything." "Why bother even trying?" "It's doomed to fail." "Your life will always suck."

The third way your survival mind operates is like a popcorn machine in which your thoughts are the popcorn, constantly pop-pop-popping up. The popcorn machine of your mind is running all the time, and it has an inexhaustible supply of corn kernels. It is designed to do nothing but create vast amounts of popcorn as quickly and efficiently as possible. What's more, which kernel of corn will pop into your mind next is random and not in your conscious control. If you struggle with a long-held belief that you are defective in some way, that schema has spawned a wide variety of habitual defectiveness thoughts, a wide selection of corn kernels that can explode and pop into your mind at any time.

One thing you may have noticed about popcorn machines is the way that the newest popcorn rises up and displaces the older popcorn. In the same way, your mind is not occupied constantly by the same thoughts. They come and go, one thought present for a moment, then replaced by the next thought.

How Defusion Helps

Defusion allows you to notice your negative thoughts as they pop up, acknowledge them, and *let them go.* As you do this, you get better and better at separating yourself from the stream of thoughts that your mind constantly generates. You develop the mental agility to sidestep thoughts of discouragement, distraction, and doubt like a soccer player evading opponents as she drives toward the goal.

When you have mastered defusion, you remember that you don't have to eat all the popcorn your mind spews out. You can't turn the popcorn machine off or keep it from popping up negative thoughts, but you *can* identify the unwholesome thoughts and leave them in the popcorn bowl. Instead of swallowing that hard, scorched, nasty piece of poor self-image, you can set it aside and say, "No thanks, mind. I'm not eating that one." Then you can wait for a more palatable thought to pop up, one more in line with your plan of valued action in your life.

Likewise, defusion helps you deal with the monsters in the back of the bus. You get better and better at letting them rave, defusing yourself from the monsters, saying to them, "Yes, I know you want me turn back and retreat. But I'm the driver—I decide where we're going next." You know that your monsters are along for the ride and that you can't get rid of them. But you don't have to let them steer. And when your salesman mind starts the hard sell, defusion helps you politely but firmly decline. You thank the sales rep for the information and do not buy into the negativity. You say, "Thanks for the information, but that is not what I need right now. I'm not interested in what you're trying to sell me."

Defusion is not a belief system or a magic trick. It's a learnable skill that improves with practice, like bookkeeping, playing volleyball, singing madrigals, or making pies. The more you practice defusion, the better you get. Let's try it now.

Exercises—Eleven Ways to Defuse

Let's get started trying out the various ways that defusion can be practiced. The rest of this chapter consists of instructions for eleven different defusion exercises. These techniques have been proven over time to work for a wide variety of depressed people who suffer from repetitive thoughts of shame and worthlessness.

Over the next two or three weeks, you should try each exercise and spend a day or two practicing it whenever your depressing thoughts start bothering you. By the time you have experimented with all eleven techniques, you will have a solid understanding of how defusion works and can continue using the techniques that work best for you. On the following page is a chart to use for keeping track of all the defusion techniques, recording when you tried them and what your personal experience of their effectiveness was.

Tracking Defusion Techniques Worksheet

Defusion technique	When I used it	Thoughts I was having	Results
Naming Your Mind			
Thanking Your Mind			
Scheduling a Time to Worry			
Sorting Thoughts into Categories			
Having (Not Being) Your Experiences			

Defusion technique	When I used it	Thoughts I was having	Results
Labeling Thoughts			
Repeating Thoughts in a Silly Voice			
Putting Thoughts on Clouds			
Objectifying Thoughts			
Physically Letting Go			
Card Carrying			

Exercise: Naming Your Mind

This is a great way to distinguish between your better self and your negative thoughts. The concept is simple: give your mind a name or nickname that is different from your own.

1. Sit or lie down in a quiet place where you won't be disturbed. Close your eyes and let your mind dwell on your typical depressing thoughts.

2. Imagine that you can hear somebody saying these thoughts out loud. Listen to the tone of voice of that person, how high or low it is. Does it sound like a man, a woman, an alien, a cartoon character? Someone you know, someone from your past, or someone you've observed in your life?

3. Give the person or character who is talking a name that is not your own. The list of possible names is almost endless. Here are some examples of names that other people have used:

    • *Sally* (named after a silly kid in Jessica's fifth-grade class)

    • *Downer Donna* (reminded Clarice of her gloomy and negative cousin Donna)

    • *Joe Blow* (Jack created a pompous, opinionated, windbag character)

    • *Mom* (because Rick's mom always predicted catastrophe)

    • *Daddy* (Susan's most distressing thoughts sounded like her dad)

    • *Muggle* (Bea was a big Harry Potter fan when she was younger)

    • *Little Bethy* (Beth's name for her most depressed, scared self)

    • *Eeyore* (named after the gloomy donkey in *Winnie the Pooh*)

4. If you are having trouble coming up with or deciding on a name, open your eyes and get a pen. Come up with five possible names for your mind's voice and write them here:

    _____

    _____

    _____

    _____

    _____

5. For the next week or so, try out different names for your mind. When the depressing thoughts start running through your mind, call your mind by name: *Hello, _____. I hear you talking again.*

6. Settle on the name you like best and see how often you notice yourself thinking in the style of that persona. In the exercises that follow, continue to call your mind by name.

By giving your mind a separate name, you remind yourself that you are more than your current train of thought. It separates you from your thoughts in a subtle but powerful way. For example, when Clarice was in the middle of ruminating on her various setbacks and disappointments, she suddenly recognized the tone of those thoughts, and she said to herself, *Oh, that sounds like Downer Donna talking. She's spouting off again, trying to bring me down.*

Thanking Your Mind

Sometimes your mind will calm down if it feels it's been heard. This defusion technique is so simple there is only one step: each time your mind pops up a defectiveness thought, say to it, *Thank you, Mind.*

Jason's depression often kept him from attending social functions. When his younger sister invited him to the christening of her new baby, he knew that he really should go, but his mind threw up all kinds of reasons why he couldn't go. As the christening day approached, he used *Thank you, Mind* to keep himself on track to attend. If we could eavesdrop on his mental dialogue with his mind on the morning of the christening, it might have sounded like this:

Mind: *Mom and Dad think I'm a loser compared to Claire.*

Jason: *Thank you, Mind.*

Mind: *She's married with a kid, and I'm a lonely basket case.*

Jason: *Thank you, Mind, for that self-defeating thought.*

Mind: *I'm so socially inept; I'll embarrass myself.*

Jason: *Thank you, Mind.*

Mind: *No one cares if I show up anyway. I could die, and they'd barely notice.*

Jason: *Thank you, Mind.*

Mind: *She's got everything. I've got nothing.*

Jason: *Thank you, Mind, for that jealous thought.*

Mind: *Not even sure I believe in baptism anymore.*

Jason: *Thank you, Mind.*

Mind: *Father Hines will ask why I haven't been to Mass or confession.*

Jason: *Thank you, Mind, for that guilty thought.*

Mind: *I don't have the right clothes anyway.*

Jason: *Thank you, Mind.*

As you can see, you can combine thanking your mind with labeling or categorizing your thoughts. By thanking his mind constantly, Jason managed to get himself to the christening. None of the catastrophes predicted by his mind came to pass. His sister Claire gave him a hug at the buffet later and whispered in his ear, "I'm so glad you came today."

Scheduling a Time to Worry

You can't control your negative thoughts, but sometimes you can schedule them, postponing them until a more convenient, less intrusive time. You can tell yourself that you will worry about your health this afternoon after class, that you will obsess about your job first thing in the morning, or that you will rage about your family's unfairness after your brother's wedding.

1. In the space below, write down three typical depressing thoughts or trigger situations that tend to lead to your defectiveness coping behaviors.

    _____

    _____

    _____

2. Write down three times in your typical day or week when it would be more convenient to entertain these depressing thoughts or think about your triggers.

_____

_____

_____

3. The next time you encounter one of these thoughts or trigger situations, tell yourself, *I'll think about this later. I'll postpone it until* _____.

Charles was obsessing about passing the exam to get his health inspector certification. Worries about failure kept popping up when he was trying to study for the exam. He planned to schedule his worrying during lunchtimes, when he would normally try to review his exam materials. The noise of the cafeteria where he ate made for poor studying anyway, so he might as well worry then. That freed his mind significantly to focus on his best time for studying, in the evening after dinner.

Sorting Thoughts into Categories

This is a good defusion technique if you enjoy an orderly turn of mind and like to analyze and categorize things.

1. As negative thoughts pass through your mind, sort them into distinct categories, such as "image," " prediction," "comparison," and so on.

2. For your categories, choose abstract nouns like "regret" or "evaluation." Avoid broad feeling words like "sad" or "mad." Here are some good categories to get you started, and there is space to add your own categories as well.

    - Prediction
    - Comparison
    - Judgment

    - Opinion
    - Theory
    - Image

- Evaluation
- Question
- Doubt
- Justification
- Assumption
- Regret

- Wish
- Memory
- _____
- _____
- _____

3. The act of categorizing will automatically distance you from your thoughts and make you more their observer and less their victim.

Jennifer imagined that she was sorting her negative thoughts into mail slots like they have at the post office. She sorted a thought about her estranged sister into the "Regret" slot. Anger over being passed up for a promotion went into "Judgment." A vision of herself twenty pounds lighter in a knockout dress went into "Image." The thought persisted, so she sorted it into "Wish" as well.

Having (Not Being) Your Experiences

This is a simple technique for taking one step back from your thoughts.

1. Whenever you have a thought that bothers you, immediately rephrase it with "I'm having the thought (or wish, judgment, etc.) that . . ." added to the beginning.

2. Here are some examples:

    - *I'm having the thought that . . . it's hopeless to try.*

    - *I'm having the expectation that . . . I will probably fail.*

    - *I'm having the evaluation that . . . nobody likes me.*

    - *I'm having the thought that . . . there's something wrong with me.*

3. Rephrasing your thoughts like this underlines the idea that thoughts are smaller than your true self, that they are something you contain or have or entertain, and that they do not have or define you. Using the "I'm having the thought that . . ." construction switches you from being fused to your thoughts to observing your thoughts.

Paolo found this technique particularly helpful when facing stressful situations like asking for more time on a term paper. When he thought, *I'm not up to this; I should just hand it in late,* he rephrased is in his mind to *I'm having the thought that I'm not up to this. I'm having the thought that I should just hand it in late.* Just taking time to rephrase his thoughts slowed down the pace of his negative thinking and allowed him to take a breath and carry on with his plan to talk to his instructor.

Labeling Thoughts

This is similar to thought sorting, but the way you visualize it in your mind is different. Instead of placing a thought in a category, you attach a label to the thought.

1. When you have a negative thought, put a label on it.

2. You can use emotional, feeling words as labels:

    •   *That was a sad thought.*

    •   *That was an angry thought.*

    •   *That was a fearful thought.*

3. You can also use more intellectual, functional, or abstract labels:

    •   *That was a judgmental thought.*

    •   *That was a self-defeating thought.*

    •   *That was a harsh thought.*

4. It helps to visualize your thoughts as objects that you are labeling. You can imagine that you are sorting through a pile of papers with the thoughts printed on them, and rubber-stamping them with labels. Or you can visualize an assembly line of mechanical parts, food items, or household objects to which you affix stickers. You are literally objectifying your thoughts instead of allowing them to objectify you.

5. Notice also how using the past tense—*was*—further distances you from your thoughts.

Mary Beth owned a storage center. She always wanted to be a sculptor, but felt she was too damaged, too unimaginative, and not worthy of a life in the arts. She often defused herself from her discouraging and regretful thoughts by labeling them:

- *That was a wishful thought.*

- *That was a self-critical thought.*

- *That was an exaggerating thought.*

- *That was a shameful thought.*

She found that filling in the blanks in a complete mental sentence slowed the pace of her thoughts, allowing her to observe them more accurately and feel more distance between her true self and her transient thought processes.

Repeating Thoughts in a Silly Voice

Your parents and teachers told you it isn't nice to make fun of people. But it's okay to make fun of your own mind in the pursuit of defusion. This may sound like a grammar school tactic, as if you are mocking yourself. But it works.

1. Do this exercise when you are alone and won't be overheard. If you do this on the bus or around people at work or school, they might think you're nuts.

2. When you notice one of your habitual depressing thoughts, say it out loud.

3. Try talking in a high, squeaky voice. Then try a low, raspy rumble. Try talking really fast or slow. Can you do a comic English butler voice? A Russian mafia voice? A horror movie villain voice? Try imitating the weird vice principal at your high school or weird Aunt Helen.

4. Experiment with tones, accents, phrasing, speed, and so on until you find a silly voice you like. The voice you settle on should make the things you typically say to yourself in your mind sound ridiculous, extreme, illogical, dumb, funny, and so on.

When Daisy tried this exercise, she used what she called her "Daisy Duck" voice. It seldom failed to lighten her mood to repeat her thoughts in a high, staccato quack:

- My life is a mess, a complete disaster.

- Nobody's ever been as wretched as me.

- I'm going to end up in a crappy trailer park like my mom.

Besides making her thoughts sound silly, Daisy noticed that expanding her mental images and one-word thoughts into complete sentences was a help. It gave her time to space out her thoughts and highlighted how exaggerated and downright silly some of those habitual thoughts were.

Putting Thoughts on Clouds

This technique focuses on the transitory nature of your thoughts, creating a vivid image of them floating away on imaginary clouds.

1. Sit or lie down in a comfortable position, in a place where you won't be disturbed by others.

2. Close your eyes and take a few slow, deep breaths into your belly.

3. Scan your body for tension, and let your muscles relax.

4. Imagine it is a warm summer day. You are watching clouds in the sky, drifting past in front of you, one after another. Notice that this takes no effort on your part. Your awareness, in which these clouds are floating, is very simple and effortless.

5. Open your mind to whatever occurs to you. As each thought, memory, image, urge, or plan arises in your mind, imagine placing it on one of the passing clouds, on which it will float away and soon be out of sight.

6. Keep putting your mental baggage on clouds that float away, reminding yourself that this is the nature of thoughts, dreams, fantasies, worries, and so on. They arise in the mind, dwell a while, and drift away. You can see the clouds float by because *you are not those clouds*. You are the *witness* of those clouds.

7. If the thought *this is stupid* or *this isn't working* occurs to you, put that thought on a cloud as well, and let it pass away.

8. If cloud imagery does not appeal to you, try imaging a string of boxcars rolling past, boxes on a conveyor belt, balloons rising into the sky and floating away, or autumn leaves in a stream floating past your position and disappearing around the bend.

Jocelyn liked the leaves-in-a-stream imagery best. Thinking about her bad grades, poor health care habits, and feelings of worthlessness, she imagined she was sitting streamside in a local park. She placed an image of her worst report card on a floating leaf and watched it drift away on the current. She put several junk food items on leaves and let them float away. She put the thought *I wish I could just die* on a leaf. As it disappeared behind a rock downstream, Jocelyn was reminded that such thoughts are temporary. They are not permanent and not a definition of her nature.

Objectifying Thoughts

This defusion technique focuses on one thought at a time, imagining it as a physical object.

1. Close your eyes for a moment and take some deep, slow breaths.

2. Choose one of your typical defectiveness thoughts.

3. If this thought were an object, what physical properties would it have?

4. Open your eyes and write down the physical properties of your thought:

    - Size _____

    - Shape _____

    - Color _____

    - Texture _____

    - Density _____

    - Consistency _____

- Weight _____

- Flexibility _____

- Temperature _____

5. Close your eyes again and visualize this object. If you are imagining this object as being inside of yourself, take it out. Place it somewhere in the room—on a table, in the middle of a rug, or whatever.

6. Imagine walking around your objectified thought. Touch it. Consider it as separate from you.

7. What did you think of this exercise? Take that thought and start over at step 4, describing it as an object of a certain size, shape, color, and so on.

When Reuben did this exercise, he imagined his thought *I can't do anything right* to be a long, skinny branching object like a dead twig from a shrub. It seemed like this object was inside his chest. He imagined taking it out of his chest. He held it in his hands, then placed it on the kitchen table, imagining the weight, the scratchy texture, the brown color, the bendy stiffness. When he had the thought, *I'm probably not doing this exercise right either,* he started over at step 4 and imagined this thought as a similar object, but smaller and a pale blue color. He removed that from his chest and put it on the table next to the original object.

Reuben was curious and fascinated by this exercise. He continued with three more thoughts, until his kitchen table was filled with spiky, different colored, gradually smaller and smaller imaginary objects. By the end, he truly appreciated that his thoughts of not doing things right were somehow separate from himself. He was the subject of his own life, and his thoughts were lesser objects.

Physically Letting Go

This kind of defusion links your thoughts to a physical gesture, automatically moving the locus of thought outside yourself and creating for it an objective reality or symbol that you can manipulate.

1. The first time you try this, do it in private, where you won't be disturbed.

2. Hold your hand out in front of you, cupped upward as if you were holding an egg or a small stone.

3. Let one of your typical depressing thoughts come into your mind.

4. When the thought is clear and complete, imagine that you are holding that thought in your outstretched, cupped hand.

5. Turn your hand over and let the thought fall away. You are consciously and symbolically letting your thought go.

6. As you go about your daily routine, you can also use this technique without anyone noticing. Just hold your hand at your side, fingers curled to hold thoughts, and turn your hand over to let them go.

When Nancy first tried this exercise, she enjoyed making it more physical. She threw thoughts away like throwing a snowball. She shook thoughts off her fingers like flinging off mud. She brushed the residue of thoughts off both hands like dust or dirt, clapping and scraping them in the classic gesture of completion: *Job well done, good riddance.* Over time, Nancy developed the habit of cupping the fingers of her left hand whenever a persistent negative thought was bothering her. She imagined placing the thought in her cupped fingers. Then she turned her hand over or just straightened her fingers, and imagined the thought crashing to the floor and disappearing. She could do this almost any time, even at work while talking to others in a meeting.

Card Carrying

Writing your distressing thoughts down on a card is another way of tying your thoughts to a tangible object that is outside of yourself.

1. Slip a pen and an index card into your pocket or purse and carry them with you tomorrow.

2. When a depressing thought about your shortcomings arises in your mind, take a moment to write it down on your card.

3. Continue to do this for each new thought that pops up. At first you might have a lot of thoughts to write on the card. The monsters on the bus love to gang up.

4. But pretty soon your thoughts will start to repeat. When you start entertaining a thought that you have already written on your card, tell yourself, *I don't have to think about this one. I've got it on the card.*

5. The effect of telling your mind *I've got it on the card!* is similar to thanking your mind. Your mind will often quiet down after you let it know that it's been heard from and noted. The monsters will cool it for a while, and you can steer the bus in relative peace.

Rick was a sales representative with a number of cold calls to make each day. When he was depressed, he would often quit early to medicate himself with a milkshake at a fast food place. He'd sit there and mull over his lousy job and unhappy life, until it was late enough to go home. Card carrying became one of Rick's favorite defusion techniques. He always carried a notebook with him anyway, so he just reserved a page in the back for disturbing thoughts. When he had a new thought to write down, he would jot it in the back of the notebook, then check his to-do list in the front and carry on with his plans for the day. Several times this kept him on track to get things done, instead of giving up and heading for a milkshake.

Conclusion

Here is Marylu's chart showing her experiences with the defusion techniques in this chapter. She was a single part-time programmer at a failing tech startup, looking for more steady work and feeling discouraged about her ability to support herself, find a satisfying relationship, and make a life in which she felt competent, secure, and "like a real person."

Marylu's Tracking Defusion Techniques Worksheet

Defusion technique	When I used it	Thoughts I was having	Results
Naming Your Mind	Monday and Tuesday	I'm not a real person. I'm insubstantial, a wisp in the wind.	Calling my mind "Whiney Wendy" felt silly. Not much help.
Thanking Your Mind	At work on Wednesday.	I'll be the first to go. They can see I don't really contribute anything worthwhile.	"Thank you, Wendy" helped a little. Thoughts came back.
Scheduling a Time to Worry	Saturday morning, while paying bills.	I'll have nothing. I'll die poor, owing money.	Really wallowed in the thoughts. Finally got tired of it and stopped.
Sorting Thoughts into Categories	At cousin Bob's graduation.	He's so far ahead of me. I'll never have a master's degree. I'm doomed to failure.	Sorting into envious, predictive, and catastrophic thoughts was distracting. Got some distance from my thoughts.
Having (Not Being) Your Experiences	Weekend at Mom's.	She's disappointed in me. I've let my family down. I'm a bad daughter.	Totally failed at this one. Completely fused to my thoughts.
Labeling Thoughts	On train to Dayton.	It's hopeless. I don't deserve love or success. Who am I kidding?	Wrote down the categories on paper, and it really worked to sort them out and get some distance.
Repeating Thoughts in a Silly Voice	On train.	It's hopeless. I don't deserve a real relationship or a decent job. I'm doomed.	Used a phony dramatic voice like a manga heroine. Cracked myself up and laughed out loud at one point.
Putting Thoughts on Clouds	At night, couldn't sleep.	Don't know what to do. Whatever I try fails. Hopeless.	Interesting. Still felt bad, but got distracted and fell asleep.

Defusion technique	When I used it	Thoughts I was having	Results
Objectifying Thoughts	Wednesday	Who would ever want me?	Made this thought a small, gray, hairy ball with a gooey center that smelled like rotten eggs. Cracked myself up again, so I guess that's good.
Physically Letting Go	In meeting, reporting on code debugging.	I'm screwing this up. They can see I'm no good. Dead weight.	Let my hand cup and open repeatedly. Was a good distraction—let me return to my topic and not get so confused.
Card Carrying	Friday, Saturday, and Sunday.	I'm worthless. What's the use? Doomed.	Completely forgot I had the cards in my purse. This one's a loser.

As you can see, Marylu tried the various techniques with various degrees of success. Her favorites were sorting thoughts into categories, labeling thoughts, and objectifying thoughts. She was less drawn to techniques like putting thoughts on clouds or objectifying thoughts. It made sense to her that she would prefer the more analytical forms of defusion, since they resembled the way her mind worked when coding software.

Marylu went on to practice her defusion techniques as she transitioned into a new job with a more viable company, where she met the person whom she eventually married. She continued to have her defectiveness thoughts, but she became more adept at defusing from them. The monsters on her bus never stopped warning her of danger and calling her names, but she persisted in steering the bus where she wanted to go.

*　*　*

Try each of the eleven defusion techniques in this chapter. It may take you a month or longer to experience them all and settle on the two or three techniques that are easier and more effective for you. Continue to use your favorites as needed. Over time, you will find that you can gain more distance between your self and your thoughts. Your use of defusion will become more habitual and more quickly deployed, so that you spend less time completely dominated by your depressing, defectiveness thoughts.

Sometimes you may find that a favorite defusion strategy fails you. That's the time to switch to another technique. From time to time, especially when the popcorn machine of your mind is really popping, come back to this chapter. Retreat to a quiet place where you won't be disturbed and run through these exercises again. Remember that defusion is a skill, like playing the piano. Defusion improves over time with practice and requires the occasional review.

Chapter 8

Avoidance and Exposure

In the last chapter, you learned how to defuse yourself from your negative thoughts. In this chapter, you will focus on the painful emotions those thoughts cause: shame, sadness, anger, fear, and so on. You will learn three important facts about these feelings:

- You can't prevent defectiveness feelings.

- You can't avoid feeling them.

- You can't change them.

You will also learn three more important facts about your negative feelings:

- You *can* observe your feelings.

- You *can* accept your feelings instead of trying to change them.

- You *can* change your behavior instead.

And with this knowledge in mind, you will do exercises to strengthen your acceptance skills, instead of struggling to avoid the unavoidable.

How You Relate to Emotional Pain

It makes sense to want to avoid emotional pain. When you start experiencing the sadness, anger, fear, and shame associated with your defectiveness schema, your first desire is to get rid of the painful feelings. You indulge in the defectiveness coping behaviors that we explored in previous chapters: lying, procrastinating, withdrawing, fantasizing—anything you can think of to avoid your feelings. But unfortunately, DCBs don't get rid of the pain.

If anything, DCBs make painful feelings worse. Jack, who'd been working on his feelings of defectiveness and shame with some success, found himself nervous about an upcoming performance evaluation at work, fearing he would be fired or have his hours cut back. He got so anxious that he avoided the situation by calling in sick the morning of the evaluation. Of course, the meeting with his supervisor was just rescheduled. Then he was late for that meeting, so that he now had absenteeism and tardiness added to the list of his work deficiencies. Jack's initial feelings of nervousness escalated to sheer panic because of his attempts to avoid them.

In this chapter, you are going to do something different. You are going to find out about the paradox of a technique called "exposure": that the best way to deal with painful feelings is to expose yourself to them, to experience them rather than trying to avoid them. You are going to observe your pain instead of trying to make it go away. You will watch your pain with mindful acceptance, without doing anything to change it, avoid it, or get rid of it.

Just to be clear, this doesn't mean that you are condoning the pain or liking it. It just means that you are acknowledging it. You are stopping to observe your experience and urges without acting on them.

The Serenity Prayer, which is used in twelve-step programs, can be helpful here:

God, grant me the serenity to accept the things I cannot change, courage to change the things I can, and wisdom to know the difference.

The things you cannot change would make a very long list, including thoughts, memories, bodily sensations, urges, impulses, the behavior of others, and all your painful emotions. The things you *can* change are your behavior and values—your actions, your choices, and what you want your life to stand for. As for the wisdom to know the difference, that's why you are working your way through this book.

For example, if you don't like the chair you're sitting in, what can you do? You can get up, carry it outside, throw it away, and get rid of it forever. You can't do that with your thoughts, memories, and feelings, because they are not tangible objects. They can't be held, touched, or permanently moved. Controlling internal experiences simply doesn't work in the same way as controlling objects in the outside world. Nevertheless, language and culture give you a lot of messages implying that you *can* control your internal experiences in the same way that you can control objects in your environment. You hear these kinds of messages all the time:

- "Calm down."

- "Don't worry."

- "Pull yourself together."

- "Chill out."

- "Where there's a will, there's a way."

As a child, you learned not to touch a hot stove, and that's a good thing. But internal pain cannot be avoided. And yet you try over and over to respond to interior pain as if it were a hot stove, as if thoughts, feelings, impulses, and sensations could actually harm you, and as if you could avoid them. But the emotions connected to your defectiveness schema are not a hot stove, and you cannot avoid them.

Exercise: The Hungry Lion—Feelings and Behavior

Try this thought experiment, which illustrates the problem with trying to control emotions. Imagine that you are in a room full of people. In a moment, a hungry lion will enter the room. This lion preys exclusively on people who feel fear or attempt to run away. The lion is incredibly sensitive and will be able to detect the slightest trace of fear that comes up in you. As long as you don't feel afraid or try to run away, you'll be completely safe, but if you experience even a trace of fear or try to run, the lion will notice this and eat you.

What would happen? You'd probably start feeling terrified. Can you control that fear? Can you make yourself not feel afraid? How about running? Do you think you could control whether you'd run? You'd probably be able to stop yourself from running, but could you stop yourself from feeling afraid?

Now think about what would happen if you knew that as long as you pet the lion, it won't eat you. What would you do? You'd probably start petting it, right? What if you knew that as long as you feed the lion, it won't eat you? You'd probably offer it some food. The point here is that controlling your behaviors and actions is different than trying to control your emotional responses. Thoughts, feelings, and sensations aren't like objects in the world. You can't move them around and control them. Your thoughts, sensations, emotions, impulses, and memories are in you, and you can't run away or escape from yourself.

Pain and suffering happen to everybody. Everyone feels disappointed, criticized, lonely, or sad at times. No one escapes these kinds of feelings. Have you ever managed to permanently remove an emotion? Have you been able to get a certain thought to never show up in your mind again? In fact, doesn't it seem that the more you don't want certain feelings and thoughts, the more you have them? The more you try to suppress your defectiveness pain or push it away with DCBs, the more intense and painful it becomes.

Card Carrying

Try this exercise over the next week:

1. Get five index cards.

2. On the front of each one, write down one of your common defectiveness thoughts, just as it occurs to you in your mind. It can be one word, a sentence, or a short paragraph—whatever will bring it vividly to mind.

3. Under the thought on each card, write the feeling that arises when you have this thought—sadness, hopelessness, fear, regret, anger, and so on.

4. On the back of each card, write a valued goal that you have for your life, something that you want to be or have or accomplish that tends to remain elusive because of your defectiveness thoughts and feelings.

5. Carry the five cards with you for a week, in your pocket or purse.

6. When you have one of your common defectiveness thoughts and feelings, remind yourself that you have it on the card, that you are in the process of noting, accepting, and living with these thoughts and feelings in order to accomplish your valued goals.

For example, Genevieve is a single, lonely, thirty-two-year-old department store clerk. She wrote these defectiveness thoughts, feelings, and goals on her five cards:

Side 1.	Side 2.
Thought: I'll never amount to anything. Feeling: Sad	Goal: I want to be promoted to assistant manager at work.
Thought: Why can't I do anything right? Feeling: Discouraged, mad at myself.	Goal: Volunteer at an animal shelter.
Thought: I'm terrible at math and science. Feeling: Hopeless, stupid.	Goal: Learn how to really use my phone.
Thought: It's better not to even try. Feeling: Depressed, stuck.	Goal: Master the inventory and returns system at work.
Thought: Everyone can see what a klutz I am. Feeling: Sad, embarrassed.	Goal: Get a better job—one working with animals.

Genevieve put her cards in the side compartment of her purse, where she also carried her phone. Every time she made or answered a call, she saw the cards and reminded herself that she could have these thoughts and feelings, while still pursuing her goals for making her life more meaningful and satisfying. At work, when she felt sad or discouraged or mad at herself, she thought, *I have this on the cards. This is what I am learning to accept as I go forward with my plans.*

Dropping the Rope

You know how some dogs love to play tug-of-war? Offer a dog the end of a short piece of rope, and it will hunker down, pulling and tugging, growling and shaking its head, pulling you around the room for as long as you want to play the game. If you stop pulling and let go of the rope, some dogs will follow you around with the rope in their mouth, trying to get you to pull some more.

Your defectiveness thoughts and the painful emotions they cause are a lot like that dog. The DCBs that you use to try to control your thoughts and feelings are a lot like playing tug-of-war with a dog. The following visualization exercise will help you explore this idea for yourself.

1. Lie down somewhere quiet, where you won't be disturbed for a few minutes. Lie on your back with your eyes closed and your arms and legs uncrossed. Close your eyes and take three slow, deep breaths.

2. Visualize your defectiveness schema as a dog. If all your thoughts about what's wrong with you were a dog, what kind of dog would they add up to? A big German shepherd? A small yappy dog? A Doberman pinscher? A mutt? In your mind's eye, build a picture of your defect dog: How big is it? How heavy? What color and markings? Imagine the sound of its bark or whine or growl. Imagine its doggy smell.

3. See yourself and your defect dog in your home, playing tug-of-war with a piece of rope. It can be white cotton sash cord or yellow plastic rope or some kind of special tug toy from the pet store. Feel the strain as you pull your end and the dog pulls back. Hear the dog panting and feel yourself getting a little short of breath as the dog pulls you around the room.

4. Imagine that you are tired of playing. It's time to start preparing dinner or dressing to go out. Let go of the rope and walk away from the dog.

5. Notice how the dog runs around in front of you with the rope in its mouth, wanting you to grab hold and tug some more. Smile at the dog and say, "Good dog, but not now."

6. Remind yourself of your surroundings, open your eyes, and get up.

When your defectiveness thoughts start pulling you around the room, when you are dragged into the sadness and hopelessness, remember this exercise. Remember that you can drop the rope. You have the option of letting go of your usual DCBs, stopping the tug-of-war, changing direction, and going on with your better plan for your day and your life.

Charlie is an insurance adjuster, recently divorced, deeply in debt, and severely affected by asthma. When he did this exercise the first time, he had been ruminating about his failed marriage, and the dog he created was an Irish setter with fur the color of his ex-wife's hair. The next time he did this exercise, he saw an English bulldog whose heft and stockiness reminded him of the weight of his financial worries. Another time, Charlie did this visualization when he was having breathing troubles, and he imagined a greyhound with skinny legs that seemed to be related to his narrow, constricted bronchi. In all three cases, Charlie told himself that he could drop the rope at will, that he did not have to be endlessly pulled around by these three representatives of his defectiveness schema.

Developing an Observer Self

This visualization exercise will help you compare your old defectiveness memories with more recent experiences to develop an observer self. The observer self is that part of you who is always there whenever you are awake, independent of transient thoughts and emotions.

1. Lie down somewhere quiet, where you won't be disturbed for a few minutes. Lie on your back with your eyes closed and your arms and legs uncrossed. Close your eyes and take three slow, deep breaths.

2. Remember a moment in the past week when your defectiveness schema was triggered. Really relive the experience by imagining where you were, who was there with you, the time of day, and the weather. Include what the scene felt like, smelled like, sounded like. Make the imagery as vivid as possible, focusing on colors, textures, sounds, and shapes.

3. What thoughts were you having? Say them out loud to yourself. What feelings came up for you last week when your defectiveness schema was triggered?

4. Now notice something really important: your self, the "I" who is observing the past event, is the same as the self in your memory. What does this mean? It means that your observer self is a constant factor. Your observer self persists, while events and thoughts and feelings change.

5. Try another memory of having your defectiveness schema triggered, one further back in time. Perhaps a memory of your parents, a caregiver, a teacher, or a friend. Once again, make the imagery as vivid as possible. Really put yourself back in that time, with all the sights, sounds, actions, smells, sensations, thoughts, and feelings.

6. Notice that this older memory also contains the same self, the same "I" observing what happened at the time, and observing the event again now, in your memory.

7. Let go of that distant memory and choose a newer, more recent event, one in which you felt good. Pick a time when you felt you were coping well, having a good time, and doing something you enjoyed or were proud of.

8. Notice that this positive memory is also being observed by your same self, the same "I." Whatever you experience or do, and whatever is done to you, it is noted by your observer self, the "I" that persists through time, through the good and the bad. This self remains the same, while events and thoughts and feelings change.

9. When you are ready, remind yourself of your surroundings and open your eyes. Get up and go on with your day, noticing the constant stability of your observer self.

When Dolores did this exercise, she lay down on the couch and relaxed. First, she visualized something that happened the day before, when she went to the gym before work. She was stretching on a mat after her workout, and on the next mat was a cute blond woman in great shape. The woman smiled at Dolores, and she smiled back. Still too shy to say anything, Dolores got up and started to head for the locker room. The other woman got up and wiped down her mat, glancing at Dolores and smiling again. Dolores felt criticized and bad, since she had not wiped down her own mat, as was gym policy. She left the gym feeling mortified, thinking, *She thinks I'm a germy slob.*

For the next part of the exercise, Dolores imagined the time a teacher in fifth grade told her that she was a "dirty little girl," because she was hoarding candy in the back of her desk, and it had attracted a swarm of ants. She remembered thinking, *I'm disgusting and nasty*, and she felt ashamed and very small, like an ant herself.

Dolores had a hard time thinking of anything recent that she had enjoyed, but finally she thought of the time last month when she surprised her arthritic mother with the gift of a new kind of jar opener. Her mother had said, "Thank you, that's so thoughtful of you!" and Dolores had felt proud out of all proportion, as if she had won a prize.

In all of these visualizations, Dolores paid attention to her observer self, the Dolores who was the common denominator of all her experiences, good and bad. She recalled the quip of a friend who once said, "Wherever you go, there you are. You can't ditch yourself." She felt a little detached, a little separate from her traumatic memories, as if they were a blazing fire, and now she had an extra layer of insulation from the scorching heat.

Conclusion

When defectiveness thoughts and painful emotions come up for you, remember that they cannot be prevented, cannot be avoided for long, and cannot be changed. What you *can* do is be willing to accept your thoughts and feelings, observe them as they occur, and carry on with your valued goals for your life. You can change your behavior, what you do in response to, and in spite of your defectiveness schema.

Chapter 9

Facing Your Shame and Sadness

You've learned a lot by now about the emotional pain your defectiveness schema stirs up. You've tried to avoid that pain by numbing and suppressing it, by using DCBs, and by trying to understand its cause (rumination). But these efforts to avoid it have only made your sadness and shame worse. In fact, avoidance has turned defectiveness-driven moments of shame or sadness into chronic depression. What might have been temporary mood states, morphing after a while into some other feeling, hardened during weeks or months of avoidance into a mood disorder. Depression is actually the direct result of trying to get away from defectiveness-driven emotional pain.

It's time to do something different when sadness and shame arise. If avoidance doesn't work over the long term, facing these emotions can offer a new and better way. To achieve this, we're introducing a technique called "emotion exposure." Instead of avoiding defectiveness-driven emotions, you'll learn to *observe* them, to ride the emotional wave, and to accept rather than resist the ebb and flow of your feelings. Exposure will help you in these ways:

- You'll learn to watch the moments of sadness and shame without getting fused with negative thoughts (rumination).

- You'll get used to your emotions rather than feeling so afraid when bouts of sadness or shame arise. And when these emotions are less fearful, you'll be less driven to engage in the old defectiveness coping behaviors (which fuel depression and make everything worse).

- You'll learn to observe your feelings and even watch your old impulses to numb and suppress *without acting on them.*

- You'll realize that emotions are time-limited, showing up in a wave-like pattern. You'll learn to watch them intensify, crest, and then slowly subside. You'll come to trust this pattern, and let the waves come and go.

Why Exposure Helps

As suggested above, emotions always show up as a wave, and like all waves, they diminish and calm—until another wave comes along. That's life—a series of emotional waves. Some difficult, some good, some big, some barely a ripple. But they all pass on their own, unless you do one or more of these three things:

- Try to block, suppress, numb, or stuff the emotional wave. Trying to stop an emotion can get you stuck at the top of the wave (Hayes, Strosahl, & Wilson, 2014).

- Act on the emotion. Research confirms that the more you get caught up in emotion-driven behavior (defectiveness coping behaviors), the stronger and more persistent the emotion becomes (Linehan, 1993; Tavris, 1989).

- Ruminate and judge yourself about why you feel bad and what's wrong with you. The more you ruminate, the worse you feel.

Exposure keeps you from blocking, ruminating, and acting on emotions, and allows you to safely ride the wave until the emotion naturally subsides. By not doing the things that make emotions worse, you learn to watch and accept feelings—until they pass. This process helps you "allow" difficult emotions, which helps you increase your tolerance of distress and also recover more quickly.

The Four Parts of an Emotion

As you begin to face your feelings, you'll notice that emotions aren't monolithic—they are made of more than one thing. There are four components of an emotion:

- **Physical sensations:** a knot in your stomach, heaviness in your chest, a flushed, hot feeling in your face, and so on.

- **Thoughts:** negative judgments about what's wrong with you and why you feel so bad.

- **Feelings:** the actual sense of sadness or shame.

- **Action urge:** what the emotion drives you to do. In the case of sadness, the action urge is often to withdraw and shut down. And with shame, the urge is typically to hide.

During exposure therapy, as you learn to observe your emotions, you'll be able to watch and distinguish all four components. Of great importance while you observe the action urge is to recognize the *moment of choice*—that exact point in time when you either slip into DCBs or choose to act on your values. Noticing each part of an emotion, as well as the moment of choice, will make a big difference in your life, because your emotions, and the behavior they unconsciously push you toward, will be transparent. You'll see what's happening, and you will have choices about it.

How to Do Emotion Exposure

An emotion exposure can be done in two ways: (1) naturally, in the present moment, as emotions are triggered in everyday life, and (2) imaginary, by using memories and images to stimulate emotional reactions from recent upsetting events. The second is the best method to use when you are first learning how to do exposure. Use the image of a recent event that really upset you and triggered your defectiveness schema to practice observing your feelings. Later, as you get more proficient, you can observe emotions as they actually show up. To do an exposure, you can record and play back the following script, or just read it—a section at a time—while following the prompts.**

1. Visualize a recent defectiveness-triggering event.

    Go back to the moment when that schema pain was triggered. Notice your surroundings; notice who is there and what that person looks like. . . . Now listen to any sounds that go with the scene, such as background noises or voices; listen to what is being said that upsets you. . . . If someone's behavior or demeanor upsets you, become aware of that. . . . Keep watching the scene and listening to what's said until you feel—right now—the schema emotion you felt at the time.

2. Notice the sensations in your body.

    Observe your physical sensations. What do you feel in your body? . . . Scan your body to see where the sensations are. . . . Imagine that each sensation has a shape and size—what are they? . . . Imagine that they each have a color—what are they? . . . What are the sensations like—a knot, a weight, a feeling of pressure?

3. Observe the feeling the event is triggering in you, describe it to yourself, and notice whether the feeling is growing or diminishing.

    Observe the feeling that goes with that upsetting scene. . . . Describe it to yourself—its intensity and quality. . . . Is it sharp or dull? . . . Could you imagine the emotion having a size . . . shape . . . color . . . texture? As you watch, see whether the emotion changes in intensity or morphs in any way. . . . Describe to yourself what you notice.

4. Notice, label, and let go of any thoughts; return to the feeling.

    As thoughts come up, just notice and label them. Say, "There's a thought." And then let it go. You don't have to get involved with it or follow where it leads. Just say, "There's a thought." . . . If you have a judgment—about yourself or another—just notice it and let it go. After noticing each thought, go back to observing your schema feeling and describing it to yourself. Notice whether it is changing in any way.

** The exercise is adapted from Matthew McKay, Patrick Fanning, Avigail Lev, and Michelle L. Skeen, *The Interpersonal Problems Workbook: ACT to End Painful Relationship Patterns* (Oakland, CA: New Harbinger Publications, 2013).

5. Notice action urges; return to describing your feeling.

   Observe any impulse to do something. . . . See whether the emotion is pushing you to take action. . . . Just be aware of the urge without doing or saying anything. . . . Let yourself watch without acting.

6. Notice blocking urges; return to describing your feeling.

   Be aware of any need to block the emotion, to push it away. But just keep describing to yourself what you feel. . . . Just stay with the feeling, noticing any changes. Is the feeling stronger? Less strong? . . . Notice where you are on the wave: ascending, cresting, receding? Are other emotions beginning to weave themselves in?

7. Stay with the exposure, describing the feeling and watching the waves until the emotion changes.

   Again notice the sensations in your body—where they are and what they feel like . . . and then notice your emotions and describe them to yourself. . . . If you have a thought, say, "There's a thought," and let it go. Just return to watching and describing your emotions. . . . If you have an impulse to avoid your feelings, notice it and return to watching the feeling. . . . If you have an impulse to say or do something, notice it and return to your feeling. . . . If the emotion is changing, let it change. . . . Just keep watching until the emotion changes in some way.

Here is a summary of the key steps for emotion exposure:

1. Visualize a recent defectiveness-triggering situation. (Skip this step for emotions that you are observing in the moment.)

2. Notice the sensations in your body.

3. Observe the feeling the event is triggering in you, describe it to yourself, and notice whether the feeling is growing or diminishing.

4. Notice, label, and let go of any thoughts; return to the feeling.

5. Notice action urges; return to describing your feeling.

6. Notice blocking urges; return to describing your feeling.

7. Stay with the exposure, describing the feeling and watching the waves until the emotion changes.

Initially, it's best to do exposure for short periods—five minutes, tops. Don't worry if the emotion doesn't morph or change in the beginning; it's enough to just get used to watching and allowing the feeling. After several *brief* exposures, push out the exposure time so you can observe the emotion shift or diminish. With each exposure, strive to accept what you feel, allowing it to wax and wane just like any emotional wave.

As you become more used to the exposure process, you can begin *present-moment exposures*—observing emotions as they arise from triggers in the course of daily life. Here's what you do: as soon as a defectiveness-based emotion gets activated, be aware of your commitment to *watch* rather than act on the feeling.

1. Notice and resist the urge to start defectiveness coping behaviors.

2. Disengage from the triggering situation as soon as you can.

3. Take time to just watch your experience. Notice the sensations in your body, the wave of feeling, the thoughts, and the urge to do something. Stay with it until you can see (1) the feeling changing in some way, and (2) the moment of choice.

4. Recall the intentions you have for values-based behavior in this situation, while also being aware of the pressure to engage in emotion-driven behavior.

5. Make a plan to act on your intention. The key is to keep observing your feelings until you have a sufficient sense of acceptance and allowing to act on your values.

• *Selma's Imagery Exposure*

Selma is a nurse in a chemotherapy infusion unit. Her work includes getting an IV started, hanging the chemotherapy meds, and monitoring her patients during the infusion process. Recently, a first-time patient forcefully complained that nobody (meaning Selma) was paying attention to her or helping her know what to expect. The angry tone was like a hard punch to Selma's defectiveness schema, and she felt an immediate surge of shame. Along with the shame was a feeling of defeat and a long chain of thoughts, like I never do anything right. *Selma tried to push the feelings away, but they clung to her, and she found herself avoiding the patient. In fact, she hardly spoke to anyone for the rest of the day.*

A few days later, Selma was ready to try emotion exposure with the feelings triggered by her patient's complaint. Her hope was that if she could face and accept the emotion, maybe it wouldn't be so crushing. Further, by learning to accept the painful surge of shame, she hoped to stay better focused on her value of compassion—rather than DCBs, such as withdrawal.

Selma started by visualizing the scene—her patient in a reclining chair with an IV line taped to her arm. She imagined the patient's angry voice and her exact words. She saw her frowning face and look of disgust. Selma kept watching the scene until the familiar burst of heat and shame rose up in her. Now she shifted the focus to her body, noticing the sensations and trying to put them into words: Heat in my chest; heat in my face; my arms are heavy—like lead pipes. Hollow feeling in my stomach, like I'm falling.

Now she observed the schema feeling: Sad. I feel like I'm bad and wrong. Humiliation. Failure. Sharp feeling—like a knife. The sadness like a fog covering me; covering everything.

She noticed her thoughts and judgments: I'm having the thought that I'm a crappy nurse. Now the thought that I don't know what I'm doing. Now the thought that I failed someone who was scared and in need. *Selma tried to let go of each thought as soon as she labeled it. She knew getting caught in them would just intensify her feelings.* Notice and let go, she reminded herself.

Next, Selma paid attention to her action urges: I want to get away, leave. I want to close up, not talk. I want to disappear. *This was the moment of choice—Selma could see that. When the patient had confronted her, she had chosen her old DCB—withdrawal—and she knew that her value of compassion would look different. She would engage; she would help.*

What were the blocking urges? I want to distract myself; think about something else. . . . I want to solve the problem rather than focus on my feelings.

Next, she went back to review everything. The sensations: My stomach still feels hollow, my arms still heavy. The feeling of heat is diminished. *Her feelings:* Sadness and humiliation, but the feeling that I'm bad is weaker. *Thoughts:* Why am I like this?

I'm having the thought that I'm screwed up. *Urges:* Hide somewhere; give up. *Her feelings again:* Sad, but also kind of resigned. I have the thought that this just happened; I have to live with it.

As Selma's exposure continued, she felt the sadness morph into an awareness of how much pain her defectiveness schema caused. She had a glimpse of compassion for herself, for how long she'd struggled. She wished she hadn't avoided her angry patient, and imagined answering her questions and trying to sooth her fear instead.

• Selma's Present-Moment Exposure

Selma's father made no secret of his hopes that she would join him in his real estate business. "You can make real money," he'd say, "instead of working for peanuts." One Sunday, when she was having lunch at her parents' house, he was at it again—asking about her student loan and suggesting she'd never make enough money to pay it off. Selma's old feelings of shame and inadequacy came roaring up. She stopped talking and shoved her plate away.

"Am I right?" he said. "You know I am." Selma gave her father a phony smile (which she knew he hated) and kept staring out the window.

After saying goodbye, Selma sat in her car and decided to face her feelings. She noticed the hot feeling in her chest, the familiar heavy feeling in her arms, and the hollowness in her abdomen. She tried to find words for her feelings: lost, sad, failure, ashamed. She noticed the thoughts: never good enough for him; never do anything right. The urge was to send him a sarcastic text: "Thanks for being such a sweet, supportive dad; so much fun visiting."

Selma was aware of her value (truth with compassion). She could have simply told him at the time that he was hurting her, rather than shut down and get passive-aggressive. Selma observed the lost, sad feeling until it began to soften into a lighter melancholy and the impulse to send the angry text faded. Instead, she sent this message: "I love you, but you're hurting me. I'm never going to do real estate. That's the truth."

Keeping an Exposure Record

As you expose yourself to defectiveness emotions, keeping a record of your progress helps you stay motivated. Whether the exposure is imaginary—using memories of a past event—or following a present-moment emotional trigger, you should document what happened. In the first column of the following Exposure Record, identify and write down the emotion you experienced. In the second column, describe, in a few words, the situation that triggered you. Note whether the exposure was imagery based (IB) or a present moment (PM) by putting an X in the appropriate column. Finally, in the last column, describe the result of the experience. (This worksheet is also available for download at http://www.newharbinger.com/45540.)

- Did you feel more accepting of the emotion?

- Did you feel less resistant and avoidant?

- Did you experience a change in the intensity or quality of the emotion—did the emotion change into something else?

- Did you become more used to the emotion—did your ability to tolerate the emotion change?

- Did you act on your urges (use DCBs), or were you able to act on values-based intentions?

- Did you feel any change in your relationship to this painful emotion? Did you feel less afraid of it?

- Did you watch and ride the emotional wave from distress to a degree of acceptance?

Exposure Record

Emotion	Trigger Situation	Exposure Type		Outcome
		IB	PM	

Emotion	Trigger Situation	Exposure Type		Outcome
		IB	PM	

• Dave's Exposure Record

Dave struggles with his defectiveness schema, which was primarily triggered in his relationship to his wife, Jenny. When Jenny asked Dave to do things, she often employed a blunt, slightly blaming style that sent Dave to the moon. He read her requests as complaints that he'd failed in some way, that whatever she wanted he should already have done. His defectiveness coping behaviors were either to get angry and defensive, or ignore her. They weren't helping the marriage, and Dave was feeling worse and worse about himself. He knew he had to face his feelings of shame and "wrongness" if he was going to act on his values (caring and support) with Jenny.

Dave's Exposure Record

Emotion	Trigger Situation	Exposure Type		Outcome
		IB	PM	
Anger, an "I'm bad" feeling	Jenny complains I'm working too late—tight, irritated voice.	x		No real change in feeling; just trying to accept it. Back and forth from anger to shame. See how shame triggers the anger.
Anger, a feeling of failure	Jenny wants the Christmas lights up—like I should have been doing it already.	x		No change in feeling. I seem to be able to stand it better. Feeling goes way back—so familiar.
Anger, an "I'm bad" feeling	Jenny worried about money—like I don't make enough.	x		I feel like shouting at her. Anger turns into a hurt feeling, a wish for her love and approval.
Hurt	She says we can't afford a lot of presents this year. I feel somehow at fault.	x		Hurt feeling fades, turns into a light sadness. I tell her I wish we could do more, and she hugs me!?

Emotion	Trigger Situation	Exposure Type		Outcome
		IB	PM	
An "I'm bad" feeling, fear	Boss complains about my travel expenses.	x		The "I'm bad" changes (surprisingly) into acceptance that he's just doing his job.
Anger, sadness	Car breaks down; Jenny complains.		x	I say, "Give me a minute." I go in the other room and just watch the feeling. Just watch it do its thing. Tell her that I'm sorry she got stranded.
An "I'm bad" feeling, hurt	Jenny says, "I wish you had more energy," which refers to my often being too tired at night for sex.	x		The hurt stays pretty strong. Eventually there's sadness, too. I decide to talk to her about how to have more fun.
Failure	Jenny looks sad after we put up the tree.		x	I go to the porch and sit with it. Feeling subsides. I ask Jenny what's making her sad.
Sadness, failure	Jenny watches children playing outside. Looks sad. We can't afford in vitro.		x	I sit with the feeling. It turns into empathy for her. I hug her; she cries. We feel (surprisingly) close.
Sadness, failure	Forgot to buy wine for Christmas Eve dinner.	x		Sadness passes. I went out and got a bottle and helped with the ham.
Anger, an "I'm bad" feeling	Jenny complains that the car is dirty.		x	I go to the garage to watch the feeling get less sharp. I wash the car.

As Dave did more exposures—particularly present-moment ones—he was increasingly able to watch the defectiveness-driven emotions without his customary coping behaviors of anger and withdrawal. Instead, as you may have noticed toward the end of his record, Dave was more often aware of the moment of choice and able to be supportive when Jenny felt sad.

Chapter 10

Self-Compassion

In the last chapter, you learned how to purposefully expose yourself to the painful feelings of defectiveness that you usually try to avoid. That was hard work. This chapter might be easier for you, because it approaches the problem of a defectiveness schema from the opposite direction, teaching you how to create positive, loving thoughts and feelings toward yourself.

The idea of self-compassion is simple: replace your usual self-critical thoughts and feelings with compassion for yourself. The results can be profound. Researcher Kristin Neff, author of *Self-Compassion* and *The Mindful Self-Compassion Workbook*, has found that developing compassion for yourself helps increase your sense of well-being as you accept your failings and imperfections, rather than taking them as irrefutable evidence of your brokenness.

Professor Paul Gilbert of the University of Derby in the United Kingdom developed a technique called "compassionate mind training," which teaches self-compassion to groups. Both Gilbert and Neff have found that self-compassion reduces feelings of depression and low self-esteem caused by an overly self-critical opinion of your abilities, traits, and worthiness.

Self-Compassion Exercises

As someone with a defectiveness schema, your default opinion of yourself is negative. The idea of self-compassion may seem far-fetched at first, but don't let that discourage you. You've come this far, and you owe it to yourself to experience this powerful intervention.

Sample each of the following exercises in turn so that you can see for yourself which ones work best for you. Start the first exercise today, and see it through for a week. Then try the second exercise, then the third, and so on, until you've tried them all. Some exercises are done just one day a week and may take an hour to complete. A couple are done a little bit every day for a week. In all, it will only take you about three weeks to experience what self-compassion has to offer to you.

Then repeat the most useful techniques over the next month or two. You'll find yourself combining and altering these methods over time, until they become a kind of personal spiritual practice, an evolving and creative habit of self-compassion.

Put Compassion into Action

- For the next week, do something compassionate and loving for yourself each day.

- Do something that you wouldn't usually do, something that constitutes a special treat for you. You might listen to music with your eyes closed, doing nothing else. Or take a walk around the block. Maybe slowly rub hand lotion all over your arms and hands. Sit somewhere quiet and have a cup of tea or fresh fruit juice. Visit a store or gallery and enjoy gazing at beautiful things.

- Don't pick things like drinking, using drugs, watching online porn, shopping, or any similar thing that you tend to overindulge in anyway. You're not trying to make your DCBs worse here.

- Tell yourself that this is a special moment, just for you. This treat is good for you, and you deserve it.

- You are expressing toward yourself the compassion and loving-kindness that you wish for all people.

When Jackson put self-compassion into action, he took the time to draw a bath instead of his usual quick shower. He relaxed in the tub and listened to his favorite old R&B song on his phone.

Compassionate Percentages

The defectiveness schema that powers your depression may feel like it applies 100 percent to everything, all the time. But that's not the case. In this self-compassion exercise, you systematically break down the percentages.

Start by answering these four questions:

- A negative trait that I see as part of my defectiveness is:

  _____

- I display this trait _____ percent of the time.

- I display this trait especially in these domains (family, relationship, parenting, friends, work, education or training, recreation, spirituality or meaning, citizenship, physical care):

  _____

- I have this trait because of these influences in my background:

  _____

Now consider these three additional questions:

- When you are not displaying this negative trait, are you the same person?

- Outside of the triggering domains, when you are not displaying this negative trait, who are you then?

- Considering your genes, your early family history, and the unavoidable traumas of life, are you entirely to blame for this negative trait?

Having considered these questions, write a more compassionate self-description that takes the percentages into account:

_____

_____

_____

Here is how Joan completed this exercise:

- A negative trait that I see as part of my defectiveness is shyness and withdrawing from people.

- I display this trait 35 percent of the time.

- I display this trait especially in these domains: with men I might become friends with, with work colleagues, and with teachers.

- I have this trait because of these influences in my background: a critical mother, absent father, super successful brother, bad breakup with Larry.

- A more compassionate self-description would be: I am shy and withdrawn only 35 percent of the time, especially with men I don't know, workmates I don't know well, and authority figures like professors. The majority of the time I am not shy, especially with my old friends and my sister Kat. This all makes sense given my introverted personality, my upbringing, and how Larry dumped me.

Exercise: Write a Love Letter to Yourself

- Pretend that you are your own best friend, a steadfast blood brother or blood sister who is always there for you, who supports you—no matter what—with unconditional love. From the point of view of that persona, use the form below to write yourself a letter.

- Start with your name. It can be your real, regular name, a nickname, or some special name that you wish a friend would call you, like "Darling" or "Dearest."

- In the next space briefly describe one of your main defectiveness schema triggers. This can be flashing back to an earlier traumatic experience, dealing with a particular family member or authority figure, contemplating an upcoming event, or any other situation that typically triggers your feelings of being less than, broken, defective, or unworthy.

- The next two spaces are for the feelings you typically have and the DCBs you have typically engaged in.

- The space labeled "However" is the most important part, where you imagine how your very best friend would express their love for you. Write from the vantage point of a person who has nothing but true compassion for you, who feels your depression and shame with you, who knows how dark it can get in your world, who understands and forgives everything, and who loves and supports you no matter what.

- Continue with the next two sections with two more trigger situations that bring up defectiveness issues for you.

- If the format of filling in blanks seems too awkward for you, write a letter in your own format. Just be sure to include the key components: your triggers, feelings, DCBs, and the statements of love, acceptance, and support.

Dear _____,

I know that when (your trigger) _____

you feel (emotions) _____

and you act this way (DCB) _____.

However, _____

_____

_____

And I know that when _____

you feel _____

and you act this way _____.

However, _____

_____

_____

And I know that when _____

you feel _____

and you act this way _____.

However, _____

_____

_____

Love,

Your Friend Forever

When your letter is done, put it away for a few hours or until the next day, and then reread it. Really take in the words and their meaning, as if you were reading them for the first time. Absorb the underlying message that, regardless of your past, your limitations, or your choices, you are worthy of love and respect.

Luanne is a clerk at the Department of Motor Vehicles, a single mother of a son with learning disabilities, and an occasional binge drinker. Here is the letter she wrote to herself:

Dear Luanne,

I know that when Mr. Sanchez at work yells at you about a mistake or how slow you are, you feel stupid, incompetent, and depressed, and you act this way: You clam up and cry.

However, I also know that you are doing your best in a hard, complicated job, helping customers who are stressed out and don't understand the system. I appreciate how you keep showing up on the job.

And I know that when Benny's school calls about his low grades and bad behavior, you feel sad and scared and like it's your fault for failing him, and you act this way: You promise them anything to get them off the line, then yell at Benny, taking it out on him instead of really helping.

However, you have honestly tried many things to help your son with his ADHD and dyslexia. You and he have been dealt a hard hand in life, dealing with serious challenges. No matter what the outcome with Benny's school is, I love and support you. I will be there for you.

And I know that when it seems like everything is weighing down on you and you will be crushed, you feel broken, shattered, and devastated, and you act this way: You call in sick, spend the day drinking and the evening sleeping it off, neglecting Benny and making everything worse.

However, I believe that at any given moment, you are doing what seems best, and sometimes you have needed to zone out for a while. You realize that calling in sick and drinking is not according to your values for you or Benny, and you are working hard to do things differently. Just know this—you can't do anything so bad that it would make me love you less. I will always be there for you.

Love,
Your Forever Friend

Compose Your Own Self-Compassion Mantra

For centuries, healers, gurus, spiritual advisors, psychologists, ministers, coaches, and motivational speakers have been touting the advantages of repeating short, positive statements to yourself. Call them what you will—mantras, slogans, pep talks, affirmations, prayers, mottoes, or mission statements—these short sayings are powerful.

Kristin Neff (2011) gives her own self-compassion mantra as an example: *This is a moment of suffering. Suffering is part of life. May I be kind to myself in this moment. May I give myself the compassion I need.* Compose your own mantra following Neff's three main points as a model—an admission of what you are suffering from, an acknowledgment that suffering cannot be avoided, and a statement of self-compassion.

What you are suffering: _____

Suffering is inevitable: _____

Your statement of compassion for yourself: _____

_____

Bernard was a middle school teacher who composed this personal self-compassion mantra:

What you are suffering: I'm feeling down about myself again.

Suffering is inevitable: It's universal to suffer these low feelings.

Your statement of compassion for yourself: This reminds me that I'm only human, and I feel compassion for myself.

When Yolanda made up her self-compassion mantra, she drew upon her experience as a knitter for vivid imagery:

What you are suffering: I feel like a sad homemade sock, ill fitting and full of dropped stitches.

Suffering is inevitable: Everybody feels like this sometimes—I'm not unique.

Your statement of compassion for yourself: I love myself and my homemade sock life.

Keep a Self-Compassion Journal

Once a day for the next seven days, write down the most depressing experience you had in the past twenty-four hours. It can be something you experienced, some information you received, or a purely mental or emotional experience. Include what happened, your thoughts, your feelings, and what you did, if anything. Finish with a compassionate response to the experience. Include these three points:

- As a human being with a defectiveness schema, I am bound to have this kind of experience.

- I can be mindful of my depressing thoughts and let them pass away, as they naturally tend to do.

- I can practice loving-kindness toward myself.

(This worksheet is also available for download at http://www.newharbinger.com/45540.)

Self-Compassion Journal

Experience	What Happened	Compassionate Response

Everett was a landscaper trying to make it in his own business. He did this exercise during a difficult week on the job. Here is how Everett completed his journal:

Experience	What Happened	Compassionate Response
Davis Street client's check bounced.	Went into a funk, thought I'm a rotten judge of character.	Everyone suffers from self-criticism. I can let it pass. I love myself.
Some tools on Ninth Street job got stolen during lunch.	Depressed—I'm incapable of taking care of myself and my things.	Everybody makes mistakes. Let it go. I accept and love myself.
Lawn on Ninth Street turned yellow. I must have over-fertilized it.	Thinking they would fire me, I lied about the "bad blight" going around, felt dishonest and dumb.	Suffering is inevitable. I'm human—I can let it go. I embrace my humanity.
Hung over, bummed out this morning.	Hit the snooze button repeatedly, moped around, late for work.	Depression happens. Wait it out. I accept myself no matter what.
Ninth Street owner called me on my "blight" lie.	I tried to cover up, but finally admitted my goof. Felt stupid.	Everyone suffers sometimes. It always passes. I feel compassion for myself.
Had to confront the guy on Davis Street, demanded cash instead of another rubber check.	Very anxious before, mad during, depressed after—a trifecta of bad feelings.	Life is gonna suck regularly. Then it unsucks for a while. Wherever I'm at on the suck cycle, I love myself.
Truck wouldn't start—dead battery. I left lights on last night.	Thought I'm so incompetent I don't deserve to live, very depressed and mad at myself.	To err is human—it's going to happen. I can wait it out, let it pass. I love myself.

• Briana's Story

Briana is an on-again off-again student who works in an art gallery. She is depressed a lot of the time. She desperately wants to be a creative artist of some kind but feels she lacks imagination. She explains, "I'm slow on the uptake. People are always laughing at some joke that I don't get. Sometimes I feel like I'm invisible, like people see right through me. Or they choose to ignore me because I'm not worth taking up space in their universe. If people were clothes, I'd be in the sale bin marked 'damaged, blemished, irregular.' "

Briana spent the month of November reading through this chapter and trying self-compassion exercises. She found that putting compassion into action was actually fun. One day she would take a warm bath after dinner and pamper herself with bubble bath. The next she mixed up some finger paint and relived her kindergarten days. Another time she went to the county museum and sketched statues in the sculpture court. She especially liked the self-indulgent activities that were creative.

The compassionate percentages exercise was not pleasant for Briana. She hated math as a kid and even the simple task of making percentages add up to one hundred was frustrating. On the other hand, she really enjoyed writing a love letter to herself. She continued to write herself little notes well past November. The act of writing "I feel real compassion toward myself" was much more meaningful to her than just saying it out loud or thinking it in her mind.

The mantra exercise also really pleased Briana. She made up several mantras, settling on this short one: I notice I am down. Getting blue will always happen. It's a signal to care for myself.

The journaling exercise was interesting, but too tedious for her to keep going for a whole week, so it would never work as a lifetime habit. In the end, Briana settled on expressing her self-compassion by occasionally pampering herself, writing herself little love notes, and using various mantras. Sometimes she still felt depressed about being damaged goods, but less frequently, less deeply, and for shorter periods of time.

Conclusion

Remember that it takes time to develop the habit of self-compassion. Do the exercises faithfully, even if you don't feel like taking the time, even if they don't seem to be working. The process of replacing self-criticism and depression with self-compassion and acceptance is a long one, full of many ups and downs along the way.

Congratulations on having reached the end of the final treatment chapters in this book. Your journey has been lengthy and challenging. You can be justly proud of yourself for persevering, and for acquiring a new understanding of defectiveness schemas and many new skills in managing your depression.

In any journey, there will be detours and doubling back. The journey of self-improvement is no exception. You can take only so many steps forward before an inevitable step backward. So the last chapter in the book is about relapse prevention. Be sure to read it and formulate a relapse plan before you put this book on the shelf.

Chapter 11

Relapse Prevention

Congratulations on completing this workbook. You have come a long way in your journey to understand and deal with your defectiveness-based depression. You identified the unique aspects of your personal defectiveness schema, explored your negative thoughts and feelings, and made a list of your most common defectiveness coping behaviors. Once you knew the size and shape of your problem, you acquired important life skills to handle it: mindfulness, acceptance, valued living, defusing from negative thoughts, healing exposure to previously avoided situations and feelings, and self-compassion.

To measure how far you have come and to celebrate your progress, complete the next two questionnaires, the Self-Care Assessment and the CES Depression Scale. Then you can compare your score with the results you got previously on these standardized assessment instruments in chapter 2.

Valued Living Questionnaire: Self-Care Assessment Part 2

In this section, please give a rating of how *consistent* your actions have been with each of your values. Please note that this is *not* asking about your ideal in each area *or* what others think of you. Everyone does better in some areas than in others. People also do better at some times than at others. *Please just indicate how you think you have been doing during the past week.* Rate each area (by circling a number) on a scale of 1 to 10. A 1 means that your actions have been *completely inconsistent with your value*. A 10 means that your actions have been *completely consistent with your value*.

During the past week, how consistent have you been with your values?

Area	completely inconsistent					completely consistent				
Family (other than marriage or parenting)	1	2	3	4	5	6	7	8	9	10
Marriage, couples, intimate relationships	1	2	3	4	5	6	7	8	9	10
Parenting	1	2	3	4	5	6	7	8	9	10
Friends and social life	1	2	3	4	5	6	7	8	9	10
Work	1	2	3	4	5	6	7	8	9	10
Education and training	1	2	3	4	5	6	7	8	9	10
Recreation and fun	1	2	3	4	5	6	7	8	9	10
Spirituality, meaning, and purpose in life	1	2	3	4	5	6	7	8	9	10
Citizenship and community life	1	2	3	4	5	6	7	8	9	10
Physical self-care (nutrition, exercise, rest, and sleep)	1	2	3	4	5	6	7	8	9	10

Total: _____

Add up the total circled numbers where 10 is the minimum and 100 is the maximum. The higher the number, the more likely you are to experience happiness in your life.

The CES Depression Scale

The CES Depression Scale (CES-D) is your final step through this chapter of self-report and introspection. Developed by the Center for Epidemiologic Studies, part of the National Institute of Mental Health, it is a thorough measure of mood. In the worksheet, complete all the prompts, add up your score, and use the interpretation key at the end to see where you fall on the spectrum.

The CES Depression Scale

Using the scale below, indicate the number that best describes how often you felt or behaved this way *during the past week.*

0 = rarely or none of the time (less than 1 day)

1 = some or a little of the time (1–2 days)

2 = occasionally or a moderate amount of the time (3–4 days)

3 = most or all of the time (5–7 days)

During the past week:

1. I was bothered by things that don't usually bother me.	
2. I did not feel like eating; my appetite was poor.	
3. I felt I couldn't shake off the blues, even with help from my family or friends.	
4. I felt that I was just as good as other people.	
5. I had trouble keeping my mind on what I was doing.	
6. I felt depressed.	
7. I felt that everything I did was an effort.	
8. I felt hopeful about the future.	

9. I thought my life had been a failure.	
10. I felt fearful.	
11. My sleep was restless.	
12. I was happy.	
13. I talked less than usual.	
14. I felt lonely.	
15. People were unfriendly.	
16. I enjoyed life.	
17. I had crying spells.	
18. I felt sad.	
19. I felt that people disliked me.	
20. I could not get going.	
Total: _____	

You can score the CES-D by *reverse-scoring* items 4, 8, 12, and 16—meaning, if your response to item 4 was "some or a little of the time," rather than giving yourself a 1, you'd give yourself a 2—and then adding up your scores for all the items. Scores will range anywhere from 0 to 60, with higher scores indicating a higher level of depression. The average score for the general population is 8. People with depression tend to score 24 or higher.

Go back to chapter 2, "Assessment," where you took these questionnaires previously. You should notice two encouraging trends:

- That these days you are acting according to your values more consistently, in more areas of your life.

- That the severity of your depression has decreased.

When Jessica compared her previously recorded scores on her Self-Care Assessment, she found that she had made progress in three important areas. First, she no longer put off her younger brother when he needed her help and support. She was in better shape herself and more able to act on her value of "love for family," spending time with her brother and coaching him on how to interview for jobs. Secondly, Jessica noticed that her focus and productivity at work was much better than in the past. It was like a veil had been lifted, and she could see solutions to problems that had plagued her for months. Finally, she felt more spiritually in tune, able to just be with herself—alone, in peace, mindful of the present, not regretting the past or worrying about the future.

Relapse Happens

It would be nice if we could tell you that your problems are now solved and that you will continue on this more comfortable plateau forever. Unfortunately, that is not the case. Life is, by definition, a series of ups and downs. Relapse happens. Your experience in the process of working through this book has undoubtedly shown you this—on some days, progress was rapid and success seemed easy, but on other days, the whole effort seemed too hard and like it would never work.

Because relapse is inevitable, because you will feel defective and depressed again some time in the future, it makes sense to have a plan for what to do about it.

Your Relapse Plan

A good relapse plan takes advantage of the new knowledge and skills you have acquired. You know the situations that are likely to trigger your defectiveness schema, the coping behaviors that you are most likely to try, and the skills you need to employ instead. So your relapse plan will have those three ingredients: trigger situations, red flag DCBs, and skilled responses.

TRIGGER SITUATIONS

You've seen these ten life domains before in this book. Refer back to chapter 2 or rely on your memory to jot down the trigger situations most likely to lead you into relapse.

Family (other than marriage or parenting) _____

_____

Marriage, couples, or intimate relationships _____

_____

Parenting _____

_____

Friends and social life _____

_____

Work _____

_____

Education and training _____

_____

Recreation and fun _____

_____

Spirituality or meaning and purpose in life _____

_____

Citizenship and community life _____

_____

Physical self-care (nutrition, excercise, rest, and sleep) _____

_____

RED FLAG DCBS

What defectiveness coping behaviors are you most likely to employ in the trigger situations above, when you start to feel your defectiveness schema kick in, and when the negative depressive thoughts start running in your mind? You can refer back to chapter 3 for this, but you can probably list these off in your sleep by now. If you need a quick reminder, here are the ten most common defectiveness coping behaviors:

Overcompensation

Aggression or hostility_____

Dominance or excessive self-assertion _____

Recognition seeking or status seeking _____

Manipulation and exploitation _____

Passive-aggressiveness or rebellion _____

Surrender

Compliance or dependence _____

Avoidance

Social withdrawal or excessive autonomy _____

Compulsive stimulation seeking _____

Addictive self-soothing _____

Psychological withdrawal _____

SKILLED REPONSES

Which of your new skills do you plan to use instead of the above DCBs? It is helpful to think in terms of long-term and short-term responses—what you can do immediately, at any time you feel the old bad feelings, as well as the long-term responses, like getting back to a weekly schedule of mindfulness meditation or another daily practice.

As a reminder, here is a table of the various skills that we've taught in this book. Mark which ones you plan to use as short-term or long-term responses.

Chapter	Skills	Short Term	Long Term
4. From Avoidance to Acceptance	New responses		
5. Mindfulness	The five senses		
	Mindful focusing		
	Mindful activities		
	The morning intention		
6. Values	Values clarification		
	Willingness		
	Commitment		
	Intention		
7. Defusion	Naming your mind		
	Thanking your mind		
	Scheduling a time to worry		
	Sorting thoughts into categories		
	Having (not being) your experiences		
	Labeling thoughts		

Chapter	Skills	Short Term	Long Term
	Repeating thoughts in a silly voice		
	Putting thoughts on clouds		
	Objectifying thoughts		
	Physically letting go		
	Card carrying		
8. Avoidance and Exposure	Serenity Prayer		
	Card carrying		
	Dropping the rope		
	Developing an observer self		
9. Facing Your Shame and Sadness	Emotion exposure		
10. Self-Compassion	Put compassion into action		
	Compassionate percentages		
	Write a love letter to yourself		
	Compose your own self-compassion mantra		
	Keep a self-compassion journal		

Putting It All Together

Use the form below to bring your relapse plan together in one document. (This worksheet is also available for download at http://www.newharbinger.com/45540.)

Relapse Plan Worksheet

Trigger Situations	Red Flag Defectiveness Coping Behaviors	Short-Term Skills	Long-Term Skills

Here is how Denise formulated her relapse plan:

Trigger Situations	Red Flag Defectiveness Coping Behaviors	Short-Term Skills	Long-Term Skills
Family dinners at Mom's, especially if Gary's there, bragging about his perfect life.	Become sarcastic and aggressive to hide my own shortcomings, feel urge to storm out and leave early.	Thank my mind, change the subject to the weather or cousins, remember valued intention.	Morning mindfulness, self-compassion walks.
Invited to parties or outings by friends.	Say I'll come and flake out, "forget" or don't show.	Observe thoughts and urges, remember intentions to value community.	Alternative response: ask what I can bring, get ingredients, make plan, put on calendar.
Finals week at school, feeling overwhelmed.	Procrastinate, rationalize that I need a break, a treat, or something else.	Observe urge to escape, physically let go, self-compassion mantra.	Carry defusion cards, morning mindfulness, get exercise and eat well.
Jack complains he doesn't get to see me, that I have no time for him.	Get angry at his "pressure" and "neediness," push him away, then feel guilty, unable to have a real relationship.	Mindfully listen to him, self-compassion mantra, make a plan calmly according to values.	Review commitment to value of close relationship.

Three weeks after she finished the exercises that became this book, Denise went to her brother Gary's birthday party at their mom's house. Gary was a successful banker and was there with his attractive wife, Cindy, and their cute daughter. Denise started to feel like a poor, unlovable failure compared to her brother. She was just about to make a sarcastic remark about people who sell out to the capitalist system when she realized that this was exactly the trigger situation she had described in her relapse plan.

Instead of lapsing back into her DCB of aggressively baiting her brother, Denise followed her plan. She used defusion to thank her mind for the negative, comparing thoughts about herself. She recalled her higher value of mindful compassion for herself and her brother. She changed the topic by asking her niece about her music lessons. And she resolved to resume her morning mindfulness meditation on the bus to school.

Conclusion

When your old feelings of shame and inadequacy return to visit you, remember your relapse plan. You no longer have to succumb to months and months of depression over your short-comings and defects. You have a new understanding and acceptance of your patterns, plus a new arsenal of skills to pull yourself out of the inevitable slumps.

We wish you good fortune in your continued efforts to live life according to your values and to meet and endure all the likely setbacks and challenges, in service to the life you choose to live each day.

Appendix 1

Worksheets

In this section, you'll find all the worksheets and exercises used in this book. You can also download them from http://www.newharbinger.com/45540.

Defectiveness Triggers Worksheet

Domain	Work	Friendship	Family	Partner	Parenting	Community
Situation						
Thoughts						
Emotions						
Urges (if you didn't react)						
Behavioral reactions						

DCB Consequence Worksheet

Domain	Work	Friendship	Family	Partner	Parenting	Community
Situation						
Thoughts						
Emotions						
Behavioral reactions						
Consequences						

New Responses Worksheet

Triggering Situation	DCB	New Alternative Responses

Defectiveness Response Profile

Most Common Feelings:

Most Common Thoughts:

Most Common Urges—DCBs:

Triggering Events Diary

Event: _____

- Emotions: _____

- Thoughts: _____

- Physical sensations: _____

- Urges: _____

- Check one: ☐ Acted on urge   ☐ Didn't act on urge

Result: _____

_____

Event: _____

- Emotions: _____

- Thoughts: _____

- Physical sensations: _____

- Urges: _____

- Check one: ☐ Acted on urge   ☐ Didn't act on urge

Result: _____

_____

Event: _____

- Emotions: _____

- Thoughts: _____

- Physical sensations: _____

- Urges: _____

- Check one: ☐ Acted on urge   ☐ Didn't act on urge

Result: _____

_____

Event: _____

- Emotions: _____

- Thoughts: _____

- Physical sensations: _____

- Urges: _____

- Check one: ☐ Acted on urge   ☐ Didn't act on urge

Result: _____

_____

Values Clarification Worksheet

Important	Domain and Value	Intention (goal)
	Intimate relationships V:	
	Parenting V:	
	Education and learning V:	
	Friends and social life V:	
	Self-care and physical health V:	
	Family of origin V:	
	Spirituality V:	

Important	Domain and Value	Intention (goal)
	Community life and citizenship V:	
	Leisure and recreation V:	
	Work and career V:	
	Other: V:	
	Other: V:	
	Other: V:	

Values Clarification Weekly Update Worksheet

Week: _____ Update

Domain and Value	Intention and Notes

Triggers and Intentions Worksheet

Shame and Defectiveness Triggers	Defectiveness Coping Behaviors	Values	Specific Intentions

Tracking Defusion Techniques Worksheet

Defusion technique	When I used it	Thoughts I was having	Results
Naming Your Mind			
Thanking Your Mind			
Scheduling a Time to Worry			
Sorting Thoughts into Categories			
Having (Not Being) Your Experiences			
Labeling Thoughts			

Defusion technique	When I used it	Thoughts I was having	Results
Repeating Thoughts in a Silly Voice			
Putting Thoughts on Clouds			
Objectifying Thoughts			
Physically Letting Go			
Card Carrying			

Exposure Record

Emotion	Trigger Situation	Exposure Type		Outcome
		IB	PM	

Emotion	Trigger Situation	Exposure Type		Outcome
		IB	PM	

Self-Compassion Journal

Experience	What Happened	Compassionate Response

Relapse Plan Worksheet

Trigger Situations	Red Flag Defectiveness Coping Behaviors	Short-Term Skills	Long-Term Skills

Appendix 2

Measures

In this section, you'll find all the assessment measures used in this book. You can also download them from http://www.newharbinger.com/45540.

Defectiveness Schema Questionnaire

The first assessment we will explore in this chapter pertains directly to the thoughts and feelings that are characteristic of your defectiveness schema. Read through the statements below, and circle T or F according to whether you think the statement is mostly true or mostly false. In cases where it's a close decision, go with your first impulse. Make sure to mark the rating that is closest to how you emotionally feel, rather than what you logically think is verifiably true. It's important to complete every item, marking either T or F (but not both), in order to get an accurate score at the end.

Statement	True	False
1. I am worthy of love and respect.	T	F
2. I often feel flawed or defective.	T	F
3. I feel okay about myself.	T	F
4. Nobody I desire would desire me if they really got to know me.	T	F
5. I have legitimate needs I deserve to fill.	T	F
6. I'm dull and boring and can't make interesting conversation.	T	F
7. I count for something in the world.	T	F
8. I'm unattractive.	T	F
9. People I like and respect often like and respect me.	T	F
10. I don't deserve much attention or respect.	T	F

Valued Living Questionnaire: Self-Care Assessment Part 1
(Wilson et al., 2010)

Below are areas of life that are valued by some people. This questionnaire will help clarify your own quality of life in each of these areas. One aspect of quality of life involves the importance you put on different areas of living. Rate the importance of each area (by circling a number) on a scale of 1 to 10. A 1 means that area is *not at all important*. A 10 means that area is *extremely important*. Not everyone will value all of these areas or value all areas the same. Rate each area according to *your own personal sense of importance*. At the end is a place for you to reflect on your responses.

Area	not at all important									extremely important
Family (other than marriage or parenting)	1	2	3	4	5	6	7	8	9	10
Marriage, couples, intimate relationships	1	2	3	4	5	6	7	8	9	10
Parenting	1	2	3	4	5	6	7	8	9	10
Friends and social life	1	2	3	4	5	6	7	8	9	10
Work	1	2	3	4	5	6	7	8	9	10
Education and training	1	2	3	4	5	6	7	8	9	10
Recreation and fun	1	2	3	4	5	6	7	8	9	10
Spirituality, meaning, and purpose in life	1	2	3	4	5	6	7	8	9	10
Citizenship and community life	1	2	3	4	5	6	7	8	9	10
Physical self-care (nutrition, exercise, rest, and sleep)	1	2	3	4	5	6	7	8	9	10

Reflection: How do you feel about this? Are there any areas that surprised you?

_____

_____

_____

Valued Living Questionnaire: Self-Care Assessment Part 2
(Wilson et al., 2010)

In this section, please give a rating of how *consistent* your actions have been with each of your values. Please note that this is *not* asking about your ideal in each area *or* what others think of you. Everyone does better in some areas than in others. People also do better at some times than at others. *Please just indicate how you think you have been doing during the past week.* Rate each area (by circling a number) on a scale of 1 to 10. A 1 means that your actions have been *completely inconsistent with your value.* A 10 means that your actions have been *completely consistent with your value.*

During the past week, how consistent have you been with your values?

Area	completely inconsistent							completely consistent		
Family (other than marriage or parenting)	1	2	3	4	5	6	7	8	9	10
Marriage, couples, intimate relationships	1	2	3	4	5	6	7	8	9	10
Parenting	1	2	3	4	5	6	7	8	9	10
Friends and social life	1	2	3	4	5	6	7	8	9	10
Work	1	2	3	4	5	6	7	8	9	10
Education and training	1	2	3	4	5	6	7	8	9	10
Recreation and fun	1	2	3	4	5	6	7	8	9	10
Spirituality, meaning, and purpose in life	1	2	3	4	5	6	7	8	9	10
Citizenship and community life	1	2	3	4	5	6	7	8	9	10
Physical self-care (nutrition, exercise, rest, and sleep)	1	2	3	4	5	6	7	8	9	10

Total: _____

Add up the total circled numbers for part 2, where 10 is the minimum and 100 is the maximum. The higher the number, the more likely you are to experience happiness in your life.

Acceptance and Action Questionnaire 2 (AAQ-2)
(Bond et al., 2011)

Below you will find a list of statements. Please rate how true each statement is for you by circling a number next to it. Use the scale below to make your choice.

1	2	3	4	5	6	7
Never true	Very seldom true	Seldom true	Sometimes true	Frequently true	Almost always true	Always true

1. My painful experiences and memories make it difficult for me to live a life that I would value.	1	2	3	4	5	6	7
2. I'm afraid of my feelings.	1	2	3	4	5	6	7
3. I worry about not being able to control my worries and feelings.	1	2	3	4	5	6	7
4. My painful memories prevent me from having a fulfilling life.	1	2	3	4	5	6	7
5. Emotions cause problems in my life.	1	2	3	4	5	6	7
6. It seems like most people are handling their lives better than I am.	1	2	3	4	5	6	7
7. Worries get in the way of my success.	1	2	3	4	5	6	7

Total: _____

Automatic Thoughts Questionnaire (ATQ)
(Hollon & Kendall, 1980)

Listed below are a variety of thoughts that pop into people's heads. Please read each thought and indicate how frequently, if at all, the thought occurred to you over the last week. Please read each item carefully and circle the appropriate answers on the answer sheet in the following fashion 1 = *not at all*, 2 = *sometimes*, 3 = *moderately often*, 4 = *often*, and 5 = *all the time*. Then, please indicate how strongly, if at all, you tend to believe that thought, when it occurs. On the right-hand side of the page, circle the appropriate answers in the following fashion 1 = *not at all*, 2 = *somewhat*, 3 = *moderately*, 4 = *very much*, and 5 = *totally*.

Items	Frequency	Degree of Belief
1. I feel like I'm up against the world.	1 2 3 4 5	1 2 3 4 5
2. I'm no good.	1 2 3 4 5	1 2 3 4 5
3. Why can't I ever succeed?	1 2 3 4 5	1 2 3 4 5
4. No one understands me.	1 2 3 4 5	1 2 3 4 5
5. I've let people down.	1 2 3 4 5	1 2 3 4 5
6. I don't think I can go on.	1 2 3 4 5	1 2 3 4 5
7. I wish I were a better person.	1 2 3 4 5	1 2 3 4 5
8. I'm so weak.	1 2 3 4 5	1 2 3 4 5
9. My life's not going the way I want it to.	1 2 3 4 5	1 2 3 4 5
10. I'm so disappointed in myself.	1 2 3 4 5	1 2 3 4 5
11. Nothing feels good anymore.	1 2 3 4 5	1 2 3 4 5
12. I can't stand this anymore.	1 2 3 4 5	1 2 3 4 5

	1 2 3 4 5	1 2 3 4 5
13. I can't get started.	1 2 3 4 5	1 2 3 4 5
14. What's wrong with me?	1 2 3 4 5	1 2 3 4 5
15. I wish I were somewhere else.	1 2 3 4 5	1 2 3 4 5
16. I can't get things together.	1 2 3 4 5	1 2 3 4 5
17. I hate myself.	1 2 3 4 5	1 2 3 4 5
18. I'm worthless.	1 2 3 4 5	1 2 3 4 5
19. I wish I could just disappear.	1 2 3 4 5	1 2 3 4 5
20. What's the matter with me?	1 2 3 4 5	1 2 3 4 5
21. I'm a loser.	1 2 3 4 5	1 2 3 4 5
22. My life is a mess.	1 2 3 4 5	1 2 3 4 5
23. I'm a failure.	1 2 3 4 5	1 2 3 4 5
24. I'll never make it.	1 2 3 4 5	1 2 3 4 5
25. I feel so helpless.	1 2 3 4 5	1 2 3 4 5
26. Something has to change.	1 2 3 4 5	1 2 3 4 5
27. There must be something wrong with me.	1 2 3 4 5	1 2 3 4 5
28. My future is bleak.	1 2 3 4 5	1 2 3 4 5
29. It's just not worth it.	1 2 3 4 5	1 2 3 4 5
30. I can't finish anything.	1 2 3 4 5	1 2 3 4 5

Total: _____

The CES Depression Scale (CES-D)

Using the scale below, indicate the number that best describes how often you felt or behaved this way *during the past week*.

0 = rarely or none of the time (less than 1 day)

1 = some or a little of the time (1–2 days)

2 = occasionally or a moderate amount of the time (3–4 days)

3 = most or all of the time (5–7 days)

During the past week:

1. I was bothered by things that don't usually bother me.	
2. I did not feel like eating; my appetite was poor.	
3. I felt I couldn't shake off the blues, even with help from my family or friends.	
4. I felt that I was just as good as other people.	
5. I had trouble keeping my mind on what I was doing.	
6. I felt depressed.	
7. I felt that everything I did was an effort.	
8. I felt hopeful about the future.	
9. I thought my life had been a failure.	
10. I felt fearful.	
11. My sleep was restless.	
12. I was happy.	
13. I talked less than usual.	
14. I felt lonely.	

15. People were unfriendly.	
16. I enjoyed life.	
17. I had crying spells.	
18. I felt sad.	
19. I felt that people disliked me.	
20. I could not get going.	
Total: _____	

A Hybrid ACT and Schema Therapy Protocol for the Treatment of Depression

The techniques and methodology used in this book were supported in part by an eight-week, quasi-experimental research study that combined the core facets of acceptance and commitment therapy (ACT) and schema focused therapy (SFT) in a group designed for individuals suffering with a defectiveness schema (Greenberg, 2017). The study found that the participants who completed the eight-week treatment demonstrated a significant decrease in depressive symptoms and an increase in overall life satisfaction. Furthermore, the findings were in line with supporting the use of a hybrid protocol in the treatment for depression, along with previous research that suggested the following:

- ACT is effective across a wide range of psychological problems, particularly depression (Hayes et al., 1999; Fledderus et al., 2012; Ruiz, 2012); and

- Maladaptive belief of defectiveness is both prominent and correlated to pathology (Calvete et al., 2005; Harris & Curtin, 2002; Schmidt & Joiner, 2004; Shah & Waller, 2000; Stopa et al., 2001).

A notable finding that contradicts the literature regarding schemas is the data from the study suggested that the schema of defectiveness was, in itself, significantly reduced from pre- to posttreatment. Studies within the domain of schema therapy have identified that one of the core features of schemas is their enduring and resilient nature to change (Stopa & Waters, 2005; Riso et al., 2006). Schema therapy, which seeks to change one's negative core beliefs, typically requires significant and extensive treatment exposure before any change can be observed. It was, therefore, hypothesized that the focus of the treatment protocol would not be to change the enduring core beliefs, but instead to help the participants bring awareness and develop better coping strategies. However, the data from this study indicated a significant reduction of endorsed belief in the schema of defectiveness. The researchers speculated that it was possible that changing the way one interacts with and responds to one's schema might reduce the believability of the schemas themselves.

The study was based on the treatment results of twenty-five individuals, separated into five groups, who were recruited from online advertisements within the area of Berkeley, California. The ethnic diversity of the participant population was 12 percent African American, 8 percent Asian, 72 percent Caucasian, and 8 percent Hispanic, with none of the five groups differing significantly in ethnicity or age. The effectiveness of the protocol was evaluated with five self-report measures (IIP-64, AAQ-2, ATQ, BDI, and VLQ) over a period of three time point assessments, pretreatment, posttreatment and one-month follow-up. The study was structured with a quasi-experimental, repeated measures design, with each of the measures using Likert scale formatting. This study hypothesized that the participants would demonstrate a significant decrease in symptomatology as measured by the reported changes in the self-assessments.

The information accumulated from the twenty-five participants over three time point measures indicated a statistically significant change from pre- to posttreatment on all of the assessments. On the IIP-64, participants demonstrated a significant decrease across all eight scales that represented one's ability not to engage in maladaptive coping behaviors in the context of their interpersonal relationships. On the ATQ, the data found that patients demonstrated a significant decline in scores from pre- to posttreatment, representing a decrease in the reported strength and frequency of automatic thoughts. On the BDI, a measure for presenting symptoms of depression, participants demonstrated a significant decrease from pre- to posttreatment. In the context of the Acceptance and Action Questionnaire (AAQ-2), participants demonstrated a greater degree of psychological flexibility with significantly lowered scores between pre- and posttreatment. On the final measure, the Valued Living Questionnaire (VLQ), participants showed an overall increase in life satisfaction, with scores elevating significantly between the pre- and posttreatment assessment phases. In short, the participants demonstrated momentous changes across all self-report scales utilized to test the effectiveness of the protocol.

The study by Greenberg (2017) was the first effort toward measuring the clinical effectiveness of the ACT/SFT hybrid protocol for the treatment of depression. Aside from the nature of limitations inherent in a pilot study—the varying group sizes (three to seven), restricted demographic sampling, and relatively low N (25)—the data and literature have clearly demonstrated the feasibility of the ACT/SFT hybrid protocol in the treatment of depression, and have served to justify a rationale for the theories and techniques you have learned throughout the course of this book.

References

Bond, F. W., Hayes, S. C., Baer, R. A., Carpenter, K. C., Guenole, N., Orcutt, H. K., Waltz, T. And Zettle, R. D. (2011). Preliminary psychometric properties of the Acceptance and Action Questionnaire – II: A revised measure of psychological flexibility and acceptance. *Behavior Therapy, 42,* 676-688.

Calvete, E., Estévez, A., López de Arroyabe, E., & Ruiz, P. (2005). The Schema Questionnaire Short Form: Structure and relationship with automatic thoughts and symptoms of affective disorders. *European Journal of Psychological Assessment, 21*(2), 90–99.

Fledderus, M., Oude Voshaar, M. A., Ten Klooster, P. M., & Bohlmeijer, E. T. (2012). Further evaluation of the psychometric properties of the Acceptance and Action Questionnaire–II. *Psychological Assessment, 24*(4), 925–936.

Gilbert, P. (2009). *The compassionate mind.* London: Constable.

Greenberg, M. (2017). *A hybrid ACT and schema therapy protocol for the treatment of depression,* Unpublished doctoral dissertation, The Wright Institute, Berkeley, CA.

Harris, A. E., & Curtin, L. (2002). Parental perceptions, early maladaptive schemas, and depressive symptoms in young adults. *Cognitive Therapy and Research, 26*(3), 405–416.

Hayes, S. C., Strosahl, K., & Wilson, K. G. (1999). *Acceptance and commitment therapy: An experiential approach to behavior change.* New York: Guilford Press.

Hayes, S. C., Strosahl, K., & Wilson, K. G. (2014). *Acceptance and commitment therapy: An experiential approach to behavior change* (2nd ed.). New York: Guilford Press.

Hollon, S. D., and Kendall, P.C. (1980). Cognitive self-statements in depression: Development of an Automatic Thoughts Questionnaire. *Cognitive Therapy and Research, 4*, 383-395.

Linehan, M. (1993). *Cognitive-behavioral treatment of borderline personality disorder.* New York: Guilford Press.

McGinn, L. K., Cukor, D., & Sanderson, W. C. (2005). The relationship between parenting style, cognitive style, and anxiety and depression: Does increased early adversity influence symptom severity though the mediating role of cognitive style? *Cognitive Therapy and Research, 29*(2), 219–242.

Neff, K. (2011). *Self-compassion: The proven power of being kind to yourself.* New York: HarperCollins.

Neff, K., & Germer, C. (2018). *The mindful self-compassion workbook: A proven way to accept yourself, build inner strength, and thrive.* New York: Guilford Press.

Riso, L. P., Forman, S. E., Raouf, M., Gable, P., Maddux, R. E., Turini-Santorelli, N., Penna, S., Blandino, J. A., Jacobs, C. H., & Cherry, M. (2006). The long-term stability of early maladaptive schemas. *Cognitive Therapy and Research, 30*(4), 515–529.

Ruiz, F. J. (2012). Acceptance and commitment therapy versus traditional cognitive behavioral therapy: A systematic review and meta-analysis of current empirical evidence. *Journal of Psychology and Psychological Therapy, 12*(2), 333–357.

Schmidt, N. B., & Joiner, T. E., Jr. (2004). Global maladaptive schemas, negative life events, and psychological distress. *Journal of Psychopathology and Behavioral Assessment, 26*(1), 65–72.

Shah, R., & Waller, G. (2000). Parental style and vulnerability to depression: The role of core beliefs. *The Journal of Nervous and Mental Disease, 188*(1), 19–25.

Stopa, L., Thorne, P., Waters, A., & Preston, J. (2001). Are the short and long forms of the Young Schema Questionnaire comparable and how well does each version predict psychopathology scores? *Journal of Cognitive Psychotherapy, 15*(3), 253–272.

Stopa, L., & Waters, A. (2005). The effect of mood on responses to the Young Schema Questionnaire: Short form. *Psychology and Psychotherapy: Theory, Research and Practice, 78*(1), 45–57.

Tavris, C. (1989). *Anger: The misunderstood emotion.* New York: Simon & Schuster.

Wilson, K. G., Sandoz, E. K., Kitchens, J., & Roberts, M. (2010) "The Valued Living Questionnaire: Defining and Measuring Valued Action within a Behavioral Framework," *The Psychological Record*: Vol. 60: Iss. 2, Article 4.

Young, J. E., Klosko, J. S., & Weishaar, M. E. (2003). *Schema therapy: A practitioner's guide.* New York: Guilford Press.

Matthew McKay, PhD, is a professor at the Wright Institute in Berkeley, CA. He has authored and coauthored numerous books, including *Self-Esteem*, *The Relaxation and Stress Reduction Workbook*, *Thoughts and Feelings*, and *ACT on Life Not on Anger*. His books combined have sold more than four million copies. He received his PhD in clinical psychology from the California School of Professional Psychology, and specializes in the cognitive behavioral treatment of anxiety and depression.

Michael Jason Greenberg, PsyD, cofacilitated a pilot study on the hybrid acceptance and commitment therapy (ACT) and schema therapy treatment protocol for defectiveness, which was developed by Matthew McKay and Michelle Skeen. He received his doctorate in clinical psychology in 2017, and holds his California licensure as a clinical psychologist. Michael has held many leadership roles, including serving as assistant department head for mental health at the Naval Hospital Twentynine Palms in Southern California, where he engaged active-duty personnel in evidence-based treatments for anxiety, depression, and post-traumatic stress disorder (PTSD).

Patrick Fanning is a professional writer in the mental health field, and founder of a men's support group in Northern California. He has authored and coauthored twelve self-help books, including *Self-Esteem*, *Thoughts and Feelings*, *Couple Skills*, and *Mind and Emotions*.

FROM OUR PUBLISHER—

As the publisher at New Harbinger and a clinical psychologist since 1978, I know that emotional problems are best helped with evidence-based therapies. These are the treatments derived from scientific research (randomized controlled trials) that show what works. Whether these treatments are delivered by trained clinicians or found in a self-help book, they are designed to provide you with proven strategies to overcome your problem.

Therapies that aren't evidence-based—whether offered by clinicians or in books—are much less likely to help. In fact, therapies that aren't guided by science may not help you at all. That's why this New Harbinger book is based on scientific evidence that the treatment can relieve emotional pain.

This is important: if this book isn't enough, and you need the help of a skilled therapist, use the following resources to find a clinician trained in the evidence-based protocols appropriate for your problem. And if you need more support—a community that understands what you're going through and can show you ways to cope—resources for that are provided below, as well.

Real help is available for the problems you have been struggling with. The skills you can learn from evidence-based therapies will change your life.

Matthew McKay, PhD
Publisher, New Harbinger Publications

If you need a therapist, the following organization can help you find a therapist trained in acceptance and commitment therapy (ACT).

Association for Contextual Behavioral Science (ACBS)
please visit www.contextualscience.org and click on *Find an ACT Therapist*.

For additional support for patients, family, and friends, please contact the following:

Anxiety and Depression Association of American (ADAA)
please visit www.adaa.org

National Alliance on Mental Illness (NAMI)
please visit www.nami.org

National Suicide Prevention Lifeline
call 24 hours a day 1-800-273-TALK (8255) or visit www.suicidepreventionlifeline.org

MORE BOOKS *from*
NEW HARBINGER PUBLICATIONS

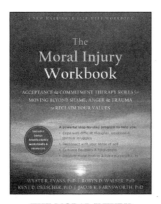

**THE MORAL INJURY
WORKBOOK**

Acceptance & Commitment Therapy
Skills for Moving Beyond Shame,
Anger & Trauma to Reclaim
Your Values

978-1684034772 / US $24.95

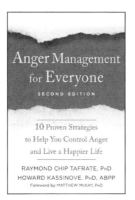

**ANGER MANAGEMENT
FOR EVERYONE,
SECOND EDITION**

Ten Proven Strategies to Help You
Control Anger & Live a Happier Life

978-1684032266 / US $17.95

Impact Publishers
An Imprint of New Harbinger Publications

**OVERCOMING UNWANTED
INTRUSIVE THOUGHTS**

A CBT-Based Guide to Getting
Over Frightening, Obsessive,
or Disturbing Thoughts

978-1626254343 / US $17.95

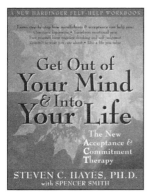

**GET OUT OF YOUR MIND
& INTO YOUR LIFE**

The New Acceptance &
Commitment Therapy

978-1572244252 / US $22.95

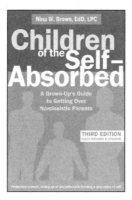

**CHILDREN OF
THE SELF-ABSORBED,
THIRD EDITION**

A Grown-Up's Guide to Getting
Over Narcissistic Parents

978-1572245617 / US $17.95

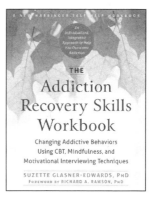

**THE ADDICTION RECOVERY
SKILLS WORKBOOK**

Changing Addictive Behaviors Using
CBT, Mindfulness & Motivational
Interviewing Techniques

978-1626252783 / US $25.95

newharbingerpublications
1-800-748-6273 / newharbinger.com

(VISA, MC, AMEX / prices subject to change without notice)

Follow Us

Don't miss out on new books in the subjects that interest you.
Sign up for our **Book Alerts** at **newharbinger.com/bookalerts**

Register your **new harbinger** titles for additional benefits!

When you register your **new harbinger** title—purchased in any format, from any source—you get access to benefits like the following:

- Downloadable accessories like printable worksheets and extra content

- Instructional videos and audio files

- Information about updates, corrections, and new editions

Not every title has accessories, but we're adding new material all the time.

Access free accessories in 3 easy steps:

1. Sign in at NewHarbinger.com (or **register** to create an account).

2. Click on **register a book**. Search for your title and click the **register** button when it appears.

3. Click on the **book cover or title** to go to its details page. Click on **accessories** to view and access files.

That's all there is to it!

If you need help, visit:

NewHarbinger.com/accessories

new harbinger
CELEBRATING
40 YEARS